What people are saying about
God Is Making Arrangements

This book is for such a time as this. People everywhere need the encouragement and insight it brings. It's a multiple witness of how God is faithful to us when coupled with our obedience to Him. The author "cannot but speak the things which (she) has seen and heard!" Acts 4:20

J. D.(Jack) Peters, aka Brother John,
producer/host of *Nite-Watch with Brother John*

This book demonstrates that we're never without hope when we realize that God is making arrangements on our behalf. Circumstances may appear hopeless, but unwavering faith in God always causes us to triumph. Thank you, Ruth, for sharing how God can and will intervene on our behalf.

Pastor Wayne Hancock,
Faith Family, Kahului, Maui

I just finished the last page of your book; I couldn't put it down! Wow! Powerful, inspiring and practical! This book declares the goodness, the power and presence of God in every-day life. If God can and will do it for Ruth, He can and will do it for you!

Pastor Diana Tripke,
Victory Life Fellowship, Kelowna, BC

This is such an inspiring book; I didn't want to put it down! It's heartwarming and filled with easy-to-read stories of a God who loves to be intimately involved in every detail of our lives. I will be giving it to those I want to encourage in their faith.

Carol Johnson,
Fort Worth, Texas

Your book challenged me to turn wishes into faith projects, to follow the still small voice of God, and trust His leading in every situation. It strengthened my awareness of His love for me as His child. Thank you for imparting such valuable truths in your book!

Ellen Redmond,
Tulsa, OK

God Is Making Arrangements

God Is Making Arrangements

Ruth Hamm

House of Ruth Publishing

GOD IS MAKING ARRANGEMENTS

Published by House of Ruth Publishing, Cochrane, AB

ISBN 978-0-9732197-0-8

Publication assistance and
digital printing in Canada by

www.pagemaster.ca

Dedication

One of the reasons for writing this book is that I want it to serve as a book of remembrance for our family and future generations and those who will be added to our family through marriage.

In the Old Testament, memorials were set up to remind God's people of events where God performed unusual feats on their behalf. Furthermore, they were instructed to tell their children the details of what had taken place at each memorial so they wouldn't forget God. That is what this book is—a series of events in my life where God did unusual things on my behalf.

I thank God for my husband, Neil, and our family, and I lovingly dedicate this to all of you.

Our children...
>   *Jennifer* and her husband Trevor Neufeld
>   *Christopher* and his wife Shannon Hamm
>   *Melanie* and her husband Michael Lingard

Our grandchildren...
>   Spencer and Brooke Neufeld
>   Sarah and Abigail Hamm
>   Michaela, Micah, Mindy and Magnum Lingard

And future generations yet to come.

Contents

Introduction

While reading through The Message version of the Bible a few years back, I came across the story of Hannah and her desperate situation. Being barren was bad enough in that day, but being taunted continually by her husband's other wife made her life almost unbearable. She went to the Temple to pour out her heart to God. Heartbroken and exhausted from crying, she could only mouth the words. The priest assumed she was drunk and reprimanded her; but instead of taking offense and adding another layer of hurt to her wounded soul, she poured out her heart to the priest. When he realized she was sober and sincere, he came into agreement with her for her prayer to be answered. It was the next sentence that jumped off the page as I read. **And God began to make arrangements according to what she had asked.**

I began to see that God had made arrangements for me throughout my whole life, even when I wasn't aware of it. I can easily trace the finger of God in sparing me from death on several occasions, in answering my childhood prayer for a good husband, in protecting my husband and family, in choosing my vocation and in providing miraculously on numerous occasions in impossible situations.

How amazing that God cared enough to track my stolen purse and its contents and put them into the hands of an honest person who would contact me. Still more amazing that the contents were found in different locations, but the most astounding part of the story is how God made arrangements for the thief to be caught by directing him to go to my sister's home. (See Chapter 7)

As I shared some of these experiences with others, whether in conversation or speaking engagements, it never ceased to amaze me how God used them to inspire others and deposit hope in the life of someone whose situation looked hopeless. The more I stepped out in faith to learn to trust God and believe that Jesus really is the same yesterday, today and forever, the more miracles began to happen in my life and family. With each step, my faith grew and I inched forward in faith to believe for greater answers to prayer.

As a result, my eyes were opened to the needs of those around me and I gained an intense longing to share the good news with others. I desired to reach out a helping hand to the weary and hopeless. I realized it was God who put that desire in me and it didn't take long for Him to provide many opportunities to do just that. Everywhere I went, I found the wounded and hurting. It was exciting to speak a word of encouragement that helped get people back on their feet and reach out in faith to God and see Him make arrangements on their behalf!

This book contains only a small portion of the many miracles in our lives. My prayer is that it will ignite a spark in the reader that will kindle a fire for God in their lives.

CHAPTER 1

Arrangements Before a Brain Hemorrhage

The emergency room nurse leaned over me with a worried expression and asked *"Mrs. Hamm, do you have a living will?"*

"No," I responded, sensing the concern in her voice. The flurry of activity and the tone in the doctor's voice as he shouted instructions to the staff confirmed that my situation was very serious. My head felt like it would explode and I fought the fear that was threatening to pull me under.

The day had started so beautifully. It was July 16, 2005, a leisurely Saturday morning. After a busy week, I relaxed by visiting the local farmer's market and attending a few garage sales. The warmth of the sun and the gentle breeze brought a sense of comfort and peace.

By early afternoon I began to feel a dull pain at the base of my skull, so I asked my husband, Neil, to pray for me. He gently placed his hand there and prayed. Normally I would have left it at that, but I felt an inward nudge to call the doctor. Because it was Saturday, my family doctor was not on call. I was told to check my blood pressure, so I drove to a local outlet to do this and found that it was somewhat elevated. I called back. She advised me to go to a smaller hospital an hour west of us because it would be a shorter wait time. *"However,"* she said, *"If it's something serious, they'll probably send you to Calgary."*

Instinctively I knew we should head east to Calgary, even though it likely meant a wait of 7-8 hours in the emergency department. By this time, the pain was increasing in intensity.

During the half hour drive, a battle took place between my mind and my spirit. My mind was telling me, *"Your father had a blood clot in the brain and lost his memory. Your mom's side of the family has a history of strokes and early death."*

My spirit battled these thoughts with scriptures that came out of my depths—scriptures that suddenly took on new meaning. It was amazing! In spite of the pain in my head, I was completely aware of the fact that I could choose which voice to entertain.

*Thou wilt keep him in perfect peace whose **mind** is stayed on thee.*[1] I couldn't remember where it was found, but it brought tremendous comfort. As I thought on that, another verse came quickly.

*For God hath not given us the spirit of fear; but of power, and of love, and of a **sound mind**.*[2] I was amazed! I had never thought of that scripture in light of keeping my mind!

I began to hum songs to drown out the fearful thoughts.

> *Peace, peace wonderful peace;*
> *Coming down from the Father above,*
> *Sweep over my spirit forever I pray,*
> *In fathomless billows of love.*[3]

Another song quickly came to mind. It seemed that a Power that was beyond me, which I knew to be the Holy Spirit, was pulling songs out of the archives of my memory, for just such a time as

---

1 Isaiah 26:3

2 2 Timothy 1:7

3 W. George Cooper/Warren D. Comell (public domain)

this. Little did I know that the battle was between life and death, and I had chosen life. Another song came to mind.

Under the blood, the precious blood
Under the cleansing, healing flood.
Keep me Savior from day to day,
Under the precious blood.[4]

It is vital that we hide God's Word in our heart so that He can use it to comfort and strengthen our faith when the need arises.

I recalled that a friend from church had miraculously recovered of a brain aneurism about two years earlier. She did not have the advantage of quoting scripture or even calling for prayer because she was unconscious. When the pastor began to pray for her the Sunday after her attack, the service turned into a prayer meeting. She had surgery to repair the aneurism and returned to work within ten weeks of being discharged. Eventually they even removed the driving restriction from her driver's license—a rarity indeed!

So I knew that God could heal, and I knew that He desires to heal. My fight was to stay in faith.

Death and life are in the power of the tongue, and they who indulge in it shall eat the fruit of it [for death or life].
Proverbs 18:21 Amplified Bible

In other words, I had a choice, and I chose life. The fact that God had done it for my friend gave me added confidence that He would do it for me.

---

4 Eliza Edmunds Stites Hewitt and William James Kirkpatrick (public domain)

I calmly called our oldest daughter who lives nearby and told her we were going to the Foothills Hospital in Calgary. She notified her two siblings as well as a close friend of mine. I knew they would pray.

Why did we choose the Foothills Hospital from the other hospitals in Calgary? I can only say I was being unconsciously led.[5]

Later a nurse told me, *"You really lucked out! You came on a Saturday, and still got the best doctor you could have had, and the Foothills is the best place you could have come for this."* I knew luck had nothing to do with it.

By the time we reached the hospital, the pain in my head was almost unbearable. I was told to wait my turn. The Emergency waiting room was filled with people, many who had been waiting for several hours. After 15 minutes or so, I was on the verge of panic because the pain was so intense. I knew I was in trouble because I never had headaches, and I could tell this was not a "normal" headache.

I went to the desk and pleaded for help. Again I was told to wait my turn. Desperate, I explained that I never got headaches and that it felt like my head would break open! She said she'd see what she could do.

After a while they put me in an examining room and left me. They told my husband to wait in the waiting room. Alone in that room, sitting on the examining table, the pain unleashed its fury. No one came, and I had no idea how long it would take for a doctor to see me. I needed help now! I cradled my head in my hands and cried out the Name that is above all names—Jesus! *"Jesus, Jesus, Jesus help me!"* I repeated it over and over, increasing in volume with each new burst of pain. It took all my determination not to give in to the fear that was trying to wrap its tentacles around my mind.

When a doctor finally came, he took my blood pressure. It was 229/126, considered extreme.[6] I was admitted immediately and things moved quickly, becoming a blur of activity. It was then that the nurse asked if I had a living will. Morphine helped dull the pain.

---

5 James 1:5

6 Normal blood pressure is considered to be 120/80.

I resisted thoughts of fear or death, but kept reminding myself of God's promises and His faithfulness. I was confident that my husband's prayer was at work, and I knew that by this time many people were praying for me—I felt carried on wings of prayer.

Within the hour they confirmed that I was having a brain hemorrhage. It was obvious that there was great concern, and yet I felt peaceful—the kind of peace that only God can give. It's not the absence of turmoil, but peace in spite of turmoil.

During the next few days I had three CT scans, an MRI and finally an angiogram. The first CT scan confirmed that it was a brain hemorrhage in the area of the brain stem—a subarachnoid hemorrhage. An MRI was ordered to get a better picture. When they still weren't satisfied, they decided to perform an angiogram. I was told that it was the "gold standard test" and would give the clearest picture.

To their delight and amazement, it indicated that the bleeding had stopped! There had been no aneurism to cause the bleeding, but rather a perforation in the blood vessel. They were unable to determine what caused it and said that it could even have been a weakness since birth. The doctor told me *"We don't know what caused it and we don't know what stopped it."* My response was *"I don't know what caused it either, but I know Who stopped it"* to which he responded, *"You're probably right."*

But I *do* know what happened. On the second day of my hospitalization, while I was praying and meditating on scripture, the word "cauterized" popped into my mind. I was rather startled because I hadn't been thinking along those lines, but I believe that the Great Physician cauterized that blood vessel and stopped the bleeding in response to all the prayers.

Our daughter, Jeni, who co-pastors with her husband Trevor, had emailed the church prayer group and those in my address book, asking them to pray and kept them updated on my progress. Within a very short time, people responded from various parts of the world and in many areas of Canada. I could literally feel the prayers, like I was being held or carried. Later I found out that a lady from church had felt led to pray for me all day Saturday, not knowing why. *It's so important to be sensitive to pray for a person when their face or name comes to mind. It can be a matter of life and death!* I am so thankful that she went out in prayer ahead of me, hours before this happened.

I stayed in the Emergency for three nights because they didn't have an available bed in a monitored area. Although I didn't know it, the battle wasn't over! There would be an attack of a different kind. But back to my story.

Spending three nights in the Emergency is like trying to sleep in a zoo. The nurses were so apologetic that I wasn't in a proper bed. They provided wonderful care, but the constant paging on the intercom, and the commotion as other emergencies arrived, made it difficult to sleep. But I was so grateful to be there; I determined to express gratitude to everyone who did anything for me, including those who swept the floors and brought the meals.

Once the pain was somewhat diminished, I became aware of what was going on in the beds around me. What an opportunity to pray for others, many of them in much worse condition than mine. Some of them had lost soundness of mind; others were in terrible pain and fear. I lay there and prayed that not one of them would go into a Christless eternity and that they would call out to God.

I remember one in particular—a young man brought in during the night. He screamed obscenities at the top of his lungs, threatening to kill the staff and their children. Every sentence was filled with curses. (When my husband worked as a part-time ambulance attendant in his youth, he said that was exactly how many people died—cursing God. What was in the heart came out of the mouth. How very tragic.)

On the fourth day, they decided to perform an angiogram later that day. By this time I was on a regular ward. At about 2:00 in the morning, I began to have the same kind of pain in the back of my head, so I rang for the nurse. She was new to me and didn't seem familiar with my case. She didn't seem concerned and brought me an ice pack to put behind my head. The other nursing staff had all stressed the importance of informing them of even the slightest pain or discomfort, so they could take my vitals and call the doctor in charge. I asked her if the ice pack could form a clot, and she said *"No, but if you want, you can just have a couple of Tylenol."* I asked her if she would at least check my blood pressure which she reluctantly did.

When she left the room, I felt concerned and didn't feel at peace about using the ice pack; she obviously didn't consult anyone, and I never saw her again. So I told the Lord, *"My confidence is in You. I don't know what's happening in my head, but You do."*

I asked the Lord to wake people to pray, and to minister rest to them as if they had slept through the night. I know of at least one person who was awakened to pray for me during that night.

My pastors had brought me a prayer cloth with three scriptures on it.

> *And God wrought special miracles by the hands of Paul: So that from his body were brought unto the sick handkerchiefs or aprons, and the diseases departed from them, and the evil spirits went out of them.*
>
> Acts 19:11 KJV

> *Jesus Christ the same yesterday, and today, and forever.*
>
> Hebrews 13:8 KJV

> *...for He [God] Himself has said, I will not in any way fail you nor give you up nor leave you without support. I will not, I will not, I will not in any degree leave you helpless nor forsake nor let you down, (relax My hold on you)! Assuredly not!*
>
> Hebrews 13:5 Amplified

I placed the prayer cloth under my head and said, *"Lord, I am going to **rest** on Your Word."* Almost immediately something supernatural happened. I felt like the Lord's hand was literally cradling my head—it was *so* comforting and soothing. From 2:30 until 6:30 that morning I had a personal encounter with the Lord unlike any I had ever had up to that time.

I felt like I was in an incubator, completely safe, warm and peaceful. It was wonderful. During the entire time, the Holy Spirit ministered scriptures to me, interpreting them to my situation. Scriptures I had known all my life took on new meaning, surprising me and bringing great comfort.

For example, I was quoting **Psalm 23**. When I got to *"Thou anointest my **head** with oil"* suddenly that verse came alive in an entirely new way. I felt a great peace.

I was reminded of Psalm 91 which I had memorized years before. I began to quote portions of it, personalizing it.

> *I dwell in the secret place of the Most High and abide under the shadow of the Almighty. **I will say** of the Lord, He is my refuge and strong tower. My God, in Him will I trust. He will cover me with His feathers and under His wings will I trust. I will not be afraid of the **terror by night**. No evil shall befall me, neither shall any plague come nigh me. A thousand may fall at my side and ten thousand at my right hand, but it shall not come nigh me. **I will call upon Him and He will deliver me**. He will be with me in trouble and will deliver me. **With long life will He satisfy me and show me His salvation**.*

I felt great comfort knowing that God had seen to it years ago that this scripture was recorded, knowing that it would bring comfort to those who experienced terror by night.

I was reminded of a few other great promises!

*Bless the Lord, O my soul, and forget not **all** His bene-fits: Who forgives all your iniquities, who heals **all** your diseases, who **redeems your life from destruction**, who **crowns you with loving kindness** and tender mercies, who satisfies your mouth with good things, so that your youth is renewed like the eagle's.*

Psalm 103:2-5 NKJV (Emphasis mine)

Be still and know that I am God. I am the Lord that healeth thee.

Psalm 46:10a KJV

Surely He has borne our griefs (sicknesses, weaknesses, and distresses) and carried our sorrows and pains [of punishment].

Isaiah 53:4a Amplified Bible

> It is vital that we hide God's Word in our heart so that He can use it to comfort and strengthen our faith when the need arises.

As I meditated on this particular verse in the dark, I had the sensation of distance, like a car driving into the distance until it disappears from view. That's what He did with my sin *and* sickness—He carried it away.

Again, I meditated on the verses on the prayer cloth. Before I knew it, four hours had passed and I felt as refreshed as if I had slept all night. I found physical and emotional strength and refreshing from that time of communion with the Lord and was sorry to see the night end because it had been so precious.

I learned a very important lesson that night, the first of four. It is vital that we hide God's Word in our heart so that He can use it to comfort and strengthen our faith when the need arises. If I had not been faithful in putting it there, it wouldn't have been there for me when I needed it. It's like a bank account—we have to make deposits in order to make withdrawals. And it pays great interest!

Later that morning they performed the angiogram[7] and Friday afternoon I was sent home feeling much improved, thinking that this was now behind me.

I had spent only a week in the hospital with a brain hemorrhage. I never lost consciousness, required no surgery and experienced no paralysis or impaired speech. All the doctors and caregivers commented on my remarkable recovery, and I used every opportunity to give God the credit because I knew I had received a miracle!

The second attack

Two days later I began to experience severe pain in my right leg and lower back. By that evening, I noticed that my right thigh and leg were really swollen, and I was unable to bend over without experiencing excruciating pain in my lower back. I was scheduled to see my family doctor the next afternoon, but again I felt an urgency not to wait. I called the answering service and they said *"Get to the hospital. It could be a blood clot."* That was at 7:30 am and by 8:30 they were performing an ultrasound which confirmed their suspicions.

They found that a fistula had developed in the groin area where the angiogram had been performed. This happens when a vein and artery begin to communicate by making a pathway toward each other. This causes the downward flow of blood to mix with the upward flow, creating turbulence, thus forming a blood clot.

I was put on strict bed rest again and faced fear the second time. Immediately the Holy Spirit began to replay in my mind the mes-

7 To create the x-ray images, your physician will inject a liquid, sometimes called "dye", through a thin, flexible tube, called a catheter. He or she threads the catheter into the desired artery or vein from an access point. The access point is usually in your groin but it can also be in your arm. This "dye", properly called contrast, makes the blood flowing inside the blood vessels visible on an x-ray. (www.vascularweb.org)

sage that my pastor had preached the day before on the importance of being convinced about what we believe.

> I had no idea that Sunday as I was listening to the message, that it was a direct word from God for me for what I would face the next day!

He told the story of Jairus who BELIEVED that if Jesus came and laid his hands on his daughter she would be healed. Jesus had already agreed to come—they were actually on their way there when He got interrupted by the woman with the issue of blood. While this lady was receiving her miracle, news came that the little girl was dead. Jesus immediately turned to Jairus and pulled him back into faith by saying *"Do not be afraid. Only believe."*

When this second attack came, I had a choice. Get into fear or get back into faith. I heard the message replayed so clearly. *"Fear not, only believe."* In other words, I couldn't fear a little and believe a little—I had to *only* believe. So that's what I did.

Here is the second lesson I learned. It's important to have a church home and be in church regularly. We don't know what's ahead of us, but God does, and He is trying to make arrangements to get the right message to us for what we will face in the coming week. It may not be sickness, but it may be a relationship problem, a financial problem or any number of things. I had no idea that Sunday as I was listening to the message, that it was a direct word from God for me for what I would face the next day!

God was making arrangements four years earlier

> It's important to obey the Holy Spirit; He's trying to protect you, not condemn you.

Although I wasn't aware of it at the time, the Lord set events in motion four years earlier. It seemed like such a gentle urging that I could easily have dismissed it. But He knows my future and was trying to make arrangements to protect me. Because I heeded His warning back then, I am alive today.

It was in August of 2001 that the Lord began to deal with me about losing 50 pounds and getting my blood pressure to a normal level. I had been on three medications for high blood pressure for over eleven years but it was still at the high end of normal.

I heard several ministers address the subject of Christians dying prematurely because they weren't looking after their health. Wholeness is our greatest witness and our body is the temple of the Holy Spirit. I came to see that it was dishonoring to expect Him to live in such a run-down "home."

> Wholeness is our greatest witness, and I saw that it was dishonoring to expect Him to live in such a run-down "home."

Although I knew it would be hard work, I obeyed and lost the weight during the next 15 months. I had so much more energy and best of all, my blood pressure was normal! My doctor was thrilled to take me off all medications and remarked *"You're an inspiration!"*

I was also very conscious about eating the right things. As a matter of fact, I had just had my annual physical with good results. I had tested my blood pressure two days before the hemorrhage and it was normal.

One of the neurologists told me *"You did all the right things. If you hadn't, we could be looking at entirely different results."*

Here's the third lesson I learned. It is vitally important to obey the Holy Spirit when He's trying to get something through to us. He's trying to protect us, not condemn us. If I wouldn't have obeyed and had died, people would have said, *"How come she wasn't healed? She believed in healing."* It wouldn't have been God's fault. His hands would have been tied because He tried to warn me.

There's a difference between conviction and condemnation. Conviction is from the Holy Spirit, and condemnation is not. Conviction is simply shining light into a dark area in order to expose something that will harm or hinder us. It's always meant for our good. Condemnation is from the enemy and it's designed to make us feel unworthy and hopeless.

> When our plans get changed, it could be that God is making arrangements to protect us!

Earlier that summer, we had made plans to spend a week with my twin brother's family at their cottage in Northern Saskatchewan the week of July 16; however, the dates were changed to accommodate everyone's schedule. Although I didn't know it, **God was making arrangements** for me. Their cottage is in a fairly remote area with no 9-1-1 service and only a very small hospital some miles away, with none of the specialists and technology available at the Foothills Hospital in Calgary.

Here's the fourth lesson I learned. Sometimes we get upset when our plans are changed unexpectedly, but we need to be sensitive and find out whether God is actually protecting us through this. He knows what's ahead, and He could be making arrangements so that we can avoid a tragedy. On the other hand, He may be positioning you to be a blessing to someone or to bring blessing into your life. The Holy Spirit can help us discern what the case may be. Just stay sensitive in your spirit and be led by peace.

Someone else's victory is dependent on yours.

I had been teaching VBS the week before the hemorrhage, acting out the Bible Expedition each day. One of the stories was of Paul and Silas in jail. We had the room darkened and the sounds playing in the background—water dripping, cell doors clanging, people shouting, etc. The kids loved it. I had them sit on the floor and bend over to touch their toes and stay in that position for awhile. I explained that this is what Paul and Silas were experiencing with their feet fastened in stocks. Then I asked them to imagine what it would be like just having been beaten, with open wounds on their back causing great pain each time they tried to move.

Then, in that situation, after being falsely accused, Paul and Silas began to sing hymns to God, and not quietly! The other prisoners heard them even though Paul and Silas were in the inner prison. Paul and Silas could have grumbled and complained, or they could have just silently tried to put up with their pain. But no, they sang hymns and brought about an earthquake that not only set them free but all the other prisoners as well! It also brought about household salvation for the jailer. How's that for turning a situation around?

Our actions and reactions in any situation affect others.

When I picked up my Bible the next morning after the four-hour visit with the Holy Spirit, it fell open to a Scripture that I had underlined many years before, but I know I was divinely directed to it that day. It was not the Bible that I usually took with me.

> *Do not fear, for I have redeemed you; I have called you by name; you are Mine! When you pass **through** the waters, I will be with you; And **through** the rivers, they will not overflow you. When you walk **through** the fire, you will not be scorched, nor will the flame burn you, for I am the Lord Your God.*
>
> Isaiah 43:2 NAS (Emphasis mine)

I was almost shouting when I read that! Years before, I had circled the words *through* because it had ministered to me then, noting the fact that God was underscoring the point by mentioning it not once, but three times! Now I was digesting it again and being renewed! God's Word is truly alive and active and powerful and energizing!

Now it was Wednesday morning and I was scheduled for a procedure to deal with the blood clot caused by the fistula. Because of the previous bleeding in the brain, the doctors did not feel comfortable giving me blood thinners to dissolve the blood clot.

The other option was to insert a stainless steel filter into my artery to "catch" the blood clot before it could reach my heart or lungs. It was necessary for me to be awake during this procedure so I could move my neck according to their instructions. The filter looked somewhat like the framework of a tiny umbrella, when collapsed. It was inserted through the jugular vein and released in the main blood vessel below the ribcage. Upon its release, it opened to "catch" any part of a clot that might travel upward toward the heart or lung.

The night before this procedure, they had told me that I must lie perfectly still because I would be "unprotected" until they could do the procedure the next morning. I told them I would be fine, knowing that I *was* protected.

The doctor told me that the only drawback to using the filter was that it had to be removed within three weeks or it must remain there permanently, requiring blood thinners for the rest of my life. Three weeks later I had it removed the same way it was inserted, and it had done its job.

I had done certain things in the natural that were helpful, like going with my instincts about getting to the hospital. But God did the supernatural like closing that perforation that caused the hemorrhage.

In actuality, God had begun to make arrangements long before this. It began in 1988 when I first became more conscious of the work of the Holy Spirit in the life of a Christian.

CHAPTER 2

Arrangements to Know the Truth

In 1988 we were hosting a home Bible study through our local church, studying the Book of Acts. We began to question why we didn't see miracles like those that happened in the early church. We didn't question if God *could*, but if He *would*.

We began to hear of people in the area who had experienced miracles and invited them to speak at our Bible Study.

I recall a big biker who gave testimony of his dramatic salvation. He shared how a little Mennonite lady brought cookies to their clubhouse on a weekly basis. She was not intimidated by them. Through her obedience, God began to make arrangements for his salvation. Eventually he became a Christian and left the gang, even though he knew the consequences. Two days before his wedding, as he was leaving his yard, a car slowly drove by. Instinctively he knew something was amiss. Five shots rang out, each one hitting the mark; but he said that before he hit the ground, he had already forgiven his attacker. Years later, his assailant also became a Christian and wrote him from prison, asking for forgiveness.

Then a couple from Manitoba, with a remarkable testimony, moved into the area. Their marriage had been in deep trouble and God miraculously healed it and began to use them in the area of deliverance.

We were beginning to see that Jesus truly is the same as when He walked on earth, and that He really is doing the same things He did back then!

> *Jesus Christ is the same yesterday, today, and forever.*
> Hebrews 13:8 NKJV

Attendance at the meetings grew until we had to find a larger meeting place. People sat on the floor, often packed in like sardines. We always began with a time of praise and worship and closed with a time of prayer. People brought their prayer requests so we spent time praying for each other and for the prayer requests.

We invited a guest speaker who taught us about the gifts of the Spirit, something we had not heard of before, but we saw it in the scriptures. He operated in the gifts of word of knowledge and word of wisdom.[8] He taught us about it from the scriptures, and then the Holy Spirit demonstrated.

He said, *"There's someone here with a problem in the lower back and God wants to heal you."* One of those people was my husband. We were amazed that, as he prayed for Neil, his back was completely healed and still is to this day! There were others with the same problem healed that night.

Then he said, *"Someone here has a problem in the neck and God will heal you tonight."* I knew he was talking about me. I had suffered with a whiplash injury for about 27 years. No amount of therapy had helped so I had just learned to live with it. It caused a grinding in my neck whenever I turned my head. As a matter of fact, the person sitting beside me could hear that grinding.

He continued on, *"If you'll just respond, God will heal you."* I raised my hand. He asked me to stand by the wall. He simply placed his hand on my head, prayed for me and asked me to turn

---

8 I Cor. 12:8 For to one is given the word of wisdom through the Spirit, to another the word of knowledge through the same Spirit.

my head. As I did, to my amazement, there was no more grinding. That's twenty-six years ago, and it's still healed!

> We learned that there's a difference between a miracle and a healing.

We were all amazed. Then he said, *"There's someone here with a lump on your back, and if you'll put your hand back there, you'll find that Jesus has healed you."*

I couldn't contain myself because our oldest daughter had just come from the chiropractor before the meeting and had a big knot on the back of her shoulder that had given her considerable pain. She reached back to touch it and found the lump was completely gone!

The Holy Spirit just continued to demonstrate. People were re-sponding in faith because they saw the results with their own eyes. *"Someone here has problems with migraine headaches. God will heal you and deliver you of them."*

My husband, Neil, had suffered with migraine headaches for over 40 years, and so did many of his siblings. Our oldest daughter had them since she was a toddler. Anyone who has experienced migraine headaches knows what a toll they take. They controlled our family. Many a family outing was cancelled because of a migraine headache. I remember having to put our three-year-old daughter in a dark room until it passed. By this time she was seventeen years old. It was not unusual for Neil to experience two or three migraines in a week, and the same with our daughter. Prior to this evening, we didn't even know that our family could be free of this.

For about a year after Neil had prayer, the headaches tried to take hold again. But he kept standing on the Word and resisting them, and eventually they just became less and less. Soon it was a month in between headaches, and then a year, and now it's been twenty-five years and we don't know what a headache is in our home. Praise God!

We learned that there's a difference between a miracle and a healing. A miracle is instantaneous whereas healing is a process. But they both come from the mighty hand of God and for that we are ever so grateful! Our body was designed to heal and that in itself should indicate that it is God's will to heal.

Our daughter was healed of headaches at the same time. Later, our son was healed of asthma and our infant grandson of eczema. One granddaughter was healed of an eye problem and another was healed of scoliosis.

Word was spreading about the miracles taking place at the Bible Study. As our confidence in God grew, we stepped out in faith to pray for people. It was not at all uncommon for the meetings to last till the wee hours of the morning. The presence of God was so strong that sometimes we silently basked in it, without anyone saying a word.

By this time we were meeting in a larger home and the lady of the house requested prayer. She had a lump in the breast and was scheduled to see a surgeon the next morning. She had previously seen a doctor who had tried to extract fluid from it, but was unable to do so. The next step was surgery.

She was a quiet person, not one to seek attention. We knew the scripture that talked about anointing with oil,[9] so we got out the cooking oil and prayed over it. Then we anointed her forehead with it and prayed for her. It was very late by the time we arrived home a half hour later.

We were just getting into bed when the telephone rang. Who would be calling at this time of night? My husband picked up the phone on the night table by his side of the bed. I could hear that it was the lady we had prayed for, but I had never heard her shouting like she was now, and I had known her for many years! I could hear it plainly. *"It's almost gone! It's almost gone!"* We were so thrilled and amazed at the same time.

---

9 James 5:13-16

The next morning she went to see the surgeon, who was also a Christian. He asked her, *"And what brings you here today?"* She replied, *"Yesterday I had a lump in my breast, but today I don't think you'll find it!"* *"And why is that?"* he asked. Her quick response was *"Because I believe the Lord healed me!"* He told her that could well be true, as he had witnessed those kinds of things before. And it was true! She never did require the surgery.

By this time, people were calling us for prayer. We saw many miracles take place and deliverances too.

An acquaintance from the small town in which we lived had called for prayer in the middle of a night. He was in a drunken, suicidal condition. Neil and our friend from Manitoba went to see him and tried to minister salvation to him, but he wasn't ready to take that step. However, they were able to get him to change his mind about suicide. We kept praying for him to accept Jesus.

One day he showed up at our door in the late afternoon. I was home alone with our children. *"I'm ready to make the decision now,"* he said. So I asked him in and led him to the Lord and prayed for his deliverance from the power of alcohol. We were just finishing when Neil arrived, and he rejoiced with us.

God did such an amazing job of delivering him, that he had absolutely no desire for alcohol. He was a changed man. We encouraged him to start coming to church, and told him that, like an infant, he needed to grow in the things of the Lord and find a church home.

He came to church periodically, but didn't heed our caution. For six months he breezed along with no desire for alcohol. He began to visit the bars with his friends just to prove to them that he didn't need to drink. As you can probably guess, he eventually fell back into his old lifestyle. We were so saddened to see this happen to him, but we had seen the power of God to deliver. However, we all have the power to choose, and there's a reason

the Bible admonishes us not to forsake the assembling of ourselves with others of like faith.[10]

Our faith continued to grow as we saw almost weekly demonstra-
tions of God's miracle-working power. Sad to say, the denomina-
tional church we had attended for nineteen years told us we must
close down the meetings and quit talking about healing. They
wanted us to go back to the way we were before. But how could
we deny our faith? With great heartache, we had to leave the
church and were shunned by church and many family members.

(On a side note, we learned so much during this time about praying for those who hurt and slandered us. We realized that the
enemy uses people and so we decided to bless instead. Many of
those people have since passed away, but I am happy to say that
the majority of those relationships have been restored).

The church we started attending had a 24 hour helpline. Members took turns answering the calls from home for any given 24
hour period. People could call anonymously for prayer in a non-
threatening environment. It was a wonderful opportunity to minister to people from all walks of life during their time of need,
whether day or night.

One afternoon I received a call from a lady who had been heavily
addicted to prescription drugs for many years. She was desperate
for freedom. I listened as she talked, and sent up a silent prayer
for the right words to say. When I asked her if I could pray for
her and assured her that God would deliver her, she was ready. I
could sense that she was drawing on every word I said, and they
were not my words—God was giving me just the right words in
answer to my silent prayer for help.

And God completely delivered her from the power of the drugs
that very day! She quit "cold turkey," and never experienced any
symptoms of withdrawal. As a result, she began to attend the
church and we talked on many occasions. Her husband, who was
not a believer, was amazed.

---

10 Hebrews 10:25

How did my journey into the supernatural power of God begin? It started in a closet!

CHAPTER 3

Arrangements in a Closet!

It was in 1984 that I began a new journey in my spiritual life. One morning while watching a Christian broadcast, the guest was talking about how she had developed a personal relationship with the Lord, and I decided to do the same thing.

Just to give you a bit of personal background, I was born into a Christian home. My dad was a pastor until I was ten years old. I never remember a time when I didn't love God, and I accepted Jesus as my Savior at an early age. I'm thankful for God's keeping power and that I never walked away from Him.

Neil and I both loved God and raised our children that way too with the limited knowledge we had at the time. However, I could see that some Christians had a deeper walk with God than I.

That day as I watched the TV program, I had a sense that what the lady was sharing was a key to my search. She shared what she had done to get alone with God, away from distractions. She literally got in her closet and prayed a simple prayer. *"Lord, I want You to talk to me and teach me. I'm going to put my own thoughts on the shelf and I'm only going to open myself up to hear Your voice. I shut out all other voices. In Jesus' Name, amen."*

So I began the next day. I sat on my son's little bench inside the bedroom closet and prayed that same prayer. I imagined my own thoughts sitting on the shelf above me, and God's thoughts being downloaded into my mind.

At that time I didn't know about Proverbs 16:3, but what a blessing it was when I discovered it years later!

> *Roll your works upon the Lord [commit and trust them wholly to Him; He will cause your thoughts to become agreeable to His will, and] so shall your plans be established and succeed.*
>
> Proverbs 16:3 Amplified Bible

But let's go back to the closet where I was waiting to hear God's voice. First, I read the Bible for a bit. Then I closed the closet door and waited. It was completely dark except for the bit of light that shone through the crack in the bi-fold door. I waited. While I waited, I thanked God for everything He had already done in my life. I recalled past victories and answers to prayer.

I had invited Him to speak to me, so in answer He gently brought to my remembrance different things that hindered my relationship with Him. I felt no condemnation, only a gentle nudge of correction. With each nudge, I repented and thanked Him for the correction. Some of the things He showed me called for further action on my part. I wrote letters and made phone calls asking for forgiveness from various people.

After some weeks of my morning visit to the closet, I felt like all was right between the Lord and me. I sensed a new depth in our relationship that didn't leave me when I left my closet. I found myself communing with Him in my thoughts throughout the day. It seemed like we were so close that He could guide me with His eye, so to speak. I got the picture in my mind of a parent who just needs to nod to a child, and the child instantly gets the message, in a nice sort of way.

I developed a hunger to read the Bible more often. I should have known this would happen. After all, the Bible reveals God's nature and character—it's His love letter to us!

I purchased a new Bible, one in which I could make notes and record personal insights I received from the Holy Spirit. I treasure it to this day. It was the Bible I had with me in the hospital when I had the brain hemorrhage. I recall at one point, I actually put it under my head and rested on the promises of God.

It was in that closet that I got my first assignment. I had no idea that God was trying to make arrangements to spare my husband's life.

Arrangements to escape a tragedy

Although I was not aware of it, the Lord was saying to me, *"Draw close to Me so I can instruct you and show you how to avoid a tragedy ahead."*

> I didn't sense any particular urgency, but because I wanted to deepen my personal relationship with God, I decided to yield to that inner impression.

I knew that His voice is usually not audible or loud; more often it's just an inner impression. That's what I felt that day. The impression I had was that I should memorize Psalms 91. However, the instructions were unusual, but very clear. I didn't sense any particular urgency, but because I wanted to deepen my personal relationship with God, I decided to yield to that inner impression. I wasn't sure that it was even God, but it did agree with the Word, and it could only benefit me. I had no idea how much!

The instructions were that I should memorize only one verse at a time, and that I was not to proceed to the second verse until the first verse was a complete reality to me. I had never memorized scripture in this fashion before, so I was excited about these instructions!

So I began. Psalms 91 KJV

Verse 1
**He that dwelleth in the secret place of the most High
shall abide under the shadow of the Almighty.**

In order to follow the instructions I had received, I needed to make it a part of my life, so I examined each word carefully to glean every possible benefit from each word.

Dwelleth: This refers to someone who has taken up residency— not someone who is visiting or dropping in from time to time. It means to stay or remain. It's that person's principal residence.

Secret place: How does a person get into a secret place? They have to know the owner, or someone who has been there, some- one who knows the password or has the key to enter. Entrance to this secret place is by invitation. God made this invitation to the entire world! No one is excluded.

Years later I wrote a poem on this subject.

The Secret Place

I sought a place of refuge from the bustle of the day,
A place where I could meditate, a place where I could pray.
I imagined a beautiful garden, with a park bench in the shade,
Where I could meet with Jesus, away from the cares of the day.

I thought of Susanna Wesley who raised such godly kids;
When she wanted to have some quiet time, this is what she did.
She sat down in her favorite chair and pulled her apron over her head.
That's how she entered the Secret Place without a word being said.

Her children quickly grew quiet; they didn't think it odd.
They knew their mother needed time to be alone with God.
I found that I could go to the Park Bench wherever I may be;
For that meeting place is in my heart—I carry it along with me.

So throughout the day, at work or play, He's just a whisper away—
To listen, counsel, laugh and advise and bless throughout my day.

And as the twilight turns to night, I rest in His loving arms;
He who watches me neither slumbers nor sleeps, so I'm safe
from all alarm.
Contentedly I fall asleep, knowing I did my part.
I got so much accomplished from The Park Bench of my heart.

©Copyright by Ruth Hamm

So how did I learn to "dwell" in that secret place? I made it a habit to "practice the presence of God." I chose to make Him a conscious part of my thoughts during all my waking hours. I kept the line of communication open all day long, trying to include Him in all my activities, asking His advice, listening for His answer. I imagined an invisible phone line connecting us, with the line open 24 hours a day. I learned that the "password" is praise! I found it in Psalms 100 in the Message Bible.

On your feet now — applaud God! Bring a gift of laughter,
Sing yourselves into his presence. Know this: God is God,
He made us; we didn't make him. We're his people, his well-
tended sheep.
Enter with the PASSWORD: "Thank you!" Make yourselves at
home, talking praise.
Thank him. Worship him. For God is sheer beauty,
All generous in love, Loyal always and ever.

(Emphasis mine)

Now that the first verse was established, I went on to the second verse.

Verse 2
I will say of the Lord, He is my refuge and my fortress:
my God; in him will I trust.

I realized that in order for this verse to become a reality in my life, I would have to start saying what it was saying and believing each word. I repeated the sentence, changing the emphasis of each word.

I will say.

I *will* say.

I will *say*.

He is my refuge and my fortress.

He *is* my refuge and my fortress.

He is *my* refuge and my fortress.

He is my *refuge* and my fortress.

He is my refuge *and* my fortress.

He is my refuge and *my* fortress.

He is my refuge and my *fortress*.

In him will I trust.

In *him* will I trust.

In him *will* I trust.

In him will *I* trust.

In him will I *trust*.

I was making a declaration. I was dedicating myself to trust Him. This was not based on a feeling—it was based on my decision to apply His Word to my life. On I went, until I had dissected the verse in every imaginable way. It reinforced my growing confidence in the Almighty.

Verse 3
Surely he shall deliver thee from the snare of the fowler, and from the noisome pestilence.

Surely. Not maybe, not sometimes, but surely! We can count on it. He *shall*, not He might.

The snare of the fowler refers to hidden traps; the noisome pestilence is a deadly disease or killing sickness, as one translation puts it.

Verse 4
He shall cover thee with his feathers, and under his wings shalt thou trust: his truth shall be thy shield and buckler.

I got a picture of myself covered by the wings of the Almighty, hidden from the view of the enemy. God's Word is Truth that we can hide in our heart. It acts as a shield to defend and protect. A shield protects the front and sides and especially the vital organs, and a buckler[11] covers all around like a bubble.

Verse 5
Thou shalt not be afraid for the terror by night; nor for the arrow that flieth by day;

I realized that we do not need to fear at all, night or day. In other words, while we are asleep, we can be confident of His protection just as we can during the daytime. This verse was especially meaningful when I was in hospital.

Did you know that Jesus was struck with terror and depression?[12] He paid the price for terror and depression so we don't have to bear it. We don't need to suffer insomnia or panic attacks, because He's always on watch, even as we sleep.

---

11 Strong's Concordance 5503 buckler: something surrounding the person, i.e. a shield:

12 Mark 14:32-34 Amplified Bible.

Then they went to a place called Gethsemane, and He said to His disciples, Sit down here while I pray. And He took with Him Peter and James and John, and began to be struck with terror and amazement and deeply troubled and depressed. And He said to them, My soul is exceedingly sad (overwhelmed with grief) so that it almost kills Me! Remain here and keep awake and be watching.

Verse 6
Nor for the pestilence that walketh in darkness; nor for the destruction that wasteth at noonday.

A pestilence is an epidemic. This verse says that we do not need to be afraid of it. We don't have to fear the latest version of the flu or other epidemics.

Verse 7

A thousand shall fall at thy side, and ten thousand at thy right hand; but it shall not come nigh thee.

> Every promise of God has to be activated personally by faith.

Even though an epidemic can take hundreds of lives all around us, we can be safe under His wings if we put our trust in Him. It has to be an active faith, not wishful thinking. It means to be absolutely convinced that we're exempt because of the price that was paid for our redemption by the Blood of Jesus. Every promise of God has to be activated personally by faith. The way we activate it is by speaking it and acting like it's true.

Verse 8
Only with thine eyes shalt thou behold and see the reward of the wicked.

We don't need to be moved by what is happening around us. Rather, we need to be moved by what God's Word says. If we stay hidden in that secret place with our trust confidently placed in Him, we are in a place of safety.

Verse 9
Because thou hast made the Lord, which is my refuge, even the most High, thy habitation;

Habitation is another word for dwelling. It's a habit to live there. A refuge is a place of safety. It's our principal residence! We are hidden in Him! In order for the enemy to get at us, he has to go through Him first. But notice that the onus is on us to make the Lord our habitation.

Verse 10
There shall no evil befall thee, neither shall any plague come nigh thy dwelling.

I was reminded of how the children of Israel were protected from the plagues and even death because they were "covered" by the blood of the lamb on their doorposts. They left Egypt with the wealth of the Egyptians in their possession in payment for all the years of slave labor. Furthermore, there wasn't a sick or even feeble person in the group! Their clothes and shoes didn't even wear out and their feet didn't swell! Their food and water was provided fresh daily! God had them covered in every area. We are "covered" by the precious blood of Jesus, with a better covenant. We need to "see" ourselves that way!

Verse 11
For he shall give his angels charge over thee, to keep thee in all thy ways.

Angelic assistance is the right of every believer according to Hebrews 1:14.[13] Notice it says "in all thy ways." If we are dwelling in the secret place, making it our habitual place of residence, we will want to walk in ways that please God. This puts us in a position to receive the benefits promised in this verse.

Verse 12
They shall bear thee up in their hands, lest thou dash thy foot against a stone.

---

13 Are they not all ministering spirits, sent forth to minister for them who shall be heirs of salvation? KJV

Having visited Israel on two occasions, this verse took on new meaning because of the abundance of stones everywhere. It wasn't difficult to imagine that dashing your foot against a stone would be a common occurrence.

Verse 13

Thou shalt tread upon the lion and adder: the young lion and the dragon shalt thou trample under feet.

This scripture agrees with Luke 10:19 that tells us we have been given all authority over all the power of the enemy and nothing shall by any means harm us. The lion is symbolic of the enemy that roars, seeking to devour. The adder, on the other hand, is stealthy and able to sneak up unseen.

> I was under the mistaken impression that if I just stayed out of Satan's way and didn't show up on his radar screen, he would leave me alone.

But this verse says that I will tread on them and trample them under my feet. Satan is under our feet. We should be putting *him* in terror, not the other way around! I heard someone say that the only thing the enemy should know about us is the size of our shoes!

We are not to be ignorant of his devices; we can and must know his method of operation and be alert so that he can't sneak up on us unawares. Hiding our head in the sand is not wise. Knowing our enemy is part of military strategy.

Up to this point in my life, I was under the mistaken impression that if I just stayed out of Satan's way and didn't show up on his radar screen, he would leave me alone. We were taught to fear him and not anger him. We didn't know that we had authority over him and that Jesus had fought him and taken the keys from him and given them to us![14]

Our position is "in Christ." If that becomes a reality to us and we are convinced of it, then we can look down on the enemy from our position of victory in Christ! Unfortunately, up to that point, I cowered in the face of the enemy, and looked up to him from a position of dread.

Let me be clear though. We don't face our enemy with arrogance and pride. The victory that we have came through Jesus. We must stay in an attitude of humility before the Lord. If we are truly hidden in Him as our Refuge and Fortress, we can shout the Word of God down to our enemy who is trying to intimidate and threaten us.

I'm reminded of the story of the boy who was being continually bullied at school and decided to take his father with him one day. He had no fear when his father was with him; he bravely confronted the bullies. We can have that same kind of confidence in our Father who will never leave us or forsake us. He's holding our hand and we're sheltered under His arm.

Verse 14
Because he hath set his love upon me, therefore will I deliver him: I will set him on high, because he hath known my name.

This is God talking! This verse describes the believer who has an intimate love relationship with God and receives the promise

---

14 In this way, he disarmed the spiritual rulers and authorities. He shamed them publicly by his victory over them on the cross. Colossians 2:15 NLT

And I will give you the keys of the Kingdom of Heaven. Whatever you forbid on earth will be forbidden in heaven, and whatever you permit on earth will be permitted in heaven. Matthew 16:19 NLT

I have told you these things, so that in Me you may have [perfect] peace *and* confidence. In the world you have tribulation *and* trials *and* distress *and* frustration; but be of good cheer [take courage; be confident, certain, undaunted]! For I have overcome the world. [I have deprived it of power to harm you and have conquered it for you.] John 16:33 Amplified of deliverance! We are seated in heavenly places[15] with Jesus because we know His name! What a position of honor we have been given. Jesus gave us power of attorney to use His Name![16]

Verse 15
He shall call upon me, and I will answer him: I will be with him in trouble; I will deliver him, and honour him.

Many Christians mistakenly believe that they should never have trouble. On the contrary, the Bible says that in this world we *will* have tribulation. But when we call upon Him and have confidence in His Name, He is with us in our time of trouble and delivers us. He's the God of more than enough, so He also honors those He delivers!

It says we will call and He will answer. There will be no busy signal, voice mail or office hours. Wireless communication originated with God! As a matter of fact, He has a toll-free number; you can find it in Jeremiah 33:3![17] His ear is always attentive to our cry.

Verse 16
With long life will I satisfy him, and shew him my salvation.

> I had no idea how soon I would have a chance to find out if the Word would really work.

By the time I had memorized this verse and applied the entire chapter to my life, I *knew* that God desires us to live our lives fully, not cut short by tragedy or sickness. Neil and I were in agreement about this, and the Word was the

---

15 ...and raised us up together, and made us sit together in the heavenly places in Christ Jesus. Ephesians 2:6 NKJV

16 And whatsoever ye shall ask in my name, that will I do, that the Father may be glorified in the Son. John 14:13 KJV

17 Call to Me, and I will answer you, and show you great and mighty things, which you do not know. Jeremiah 33:3 NKJV

basis for our confidence. I had no idea how soon I would have a chance to find out if the Word would really work.

CHAPTER 4

Arrangements For Protection

"I'm going to kill your husband!"

I was at work when I got the call from one of Neil's employees. *"Get to the hospital quickly. Neil has fallen on his head and lost his memory."* I hung up the telephone and calmly prepared for the ten-mile trip to Saskatoon. My co-workers, thinking I was in shock, insisted I call a friend to drive me there. Finally, to put them at ease, I agreed.

I made a bold declaration to my co-workers. *"I believe that by the time I get to the hospital, not only will Neil have his memory restored, but it will be seven times better than it was before!"* I recalled a scripture that says if a thief is caught, he must pay back seven times what he took.

> *"But if he be found, he shall restore sevenfold."*
>
> Proverbs 6:30 KJV

I was amazed at the peace I was experiencing! There was no fear, just a confidence in knowing that all was well. God's Word was hidden in my heart and I knew it was true! I was convinced that God would keep His Word.

If this call had come several months earlier, my reaction would have set in motion a different set of circumstances. I have no doubt that I would have become a widow that day if I had not heeded the prompting of the Holy Spirit in my closet some months before to memorize Psalm 91.

The dream

About two weeks before I received this call, I had a dream that could have been very disturbing if it had come a month earlier. It was the beginning of December—the dream seemed so real that at first I had difficulty discerning whether I was awake or asleep. In the dream, the devil came to me and said, *"I'm going to kill your husband."* My immediate response was *"Oh no, you're not; I take authority over you in the Name of Jesus."* At the mention of that Name, he fled. Amazingly, I had no fear in the dream or when I awakened.

In the morning I shared the dream with Neil and we joined hands and agreed that any attempt on his life would be unsuccessful.

I'm building your husband's coffin!

> I realized that the devil can borrow the mouth of a Christian, like he did with Peter.

The next morning we decided to go to Saskatoon to do some Christmas shopping. Before we left, my husband wanted to give some last-minute instructions to his employee in the workshop. When we entered the shop, the employee looked up and said to me, *"I'm building your husband's coffin."* To say we were shocked would be an understatement! This man was a believer, and it was totally out of character for him to say something of that nature. I replied, *"Oh no, you're not! My husband isn't going to need a coffin now, nor for many years to come!"*

I realized that the devil can borrow the mouth of a Christian, like he did with Peter in Matthew 16:22, 23 NKJV.

> *Then Peter took Him aside and began to rebuke Him, saying, "Far be it from You, Lord; this shall not happen to You!" (Notice Jesus' response.) But He turned and said to Peter, "Get behind Me, Satan! You are an offense to Me, for you are not mindful of the things of God, but the things of men."*

It was *Peter's mouth* doing the speaking, but God did not inspire the words. The devil simply borrowed Peter's mouth for a bit! And Jesus addressed Satan, not Peter.

We left the shop and got in our vehicle; but before we left, we again held hands and broke the power of those words in Jesus' Name! We realized that the enemy was trying to paint a picture for us, a picture of destruction. We had the choice to receive that picture as truth, or to denounce it as a lie.

Two weeks after the incident in the workshop, the call came from the hospital.

I was told that Neil had lost his memory, that he had a serious concussion and didn't know where he was or why. He kept repeating the same questions over and over. This report was totally contrary to what I believed. I knew that the doctors would do all they could, and so would God!

It looked as though someone had tied a rope around Neil's ankles and pulled his feet from under him.

Don't get me wrong. I was not denying the fact that this was the present condition, but I was denying it the right to remain that way.

We arrived at the hospital in less than an hour of the call, where I met our employee who told me what had happened. He was a believer who knew how to pray effectively. I thank God that he was with Neil when it happened. By the way, this was not the same employee who said he was building Neil's coffin.

They had been walking to the vehicle across an icy parking lot. (In his youth, my husband was a steel climber and had a reputation for being steady on his feet.) The employee said it looked as though someone had tied a rope around Neil's ankles and pulled his feet from under him. When he fell, the back of his head hit the ice with great force, resulting in a serious concussion. The employee knew this was no ordinary fall and immediately laid hands on him and prayed and then took him to the hospital.

When I entered the room, Neil greeted me and I knew that he was already whole, just like I had declared. God was honoring His Word. The doctor, however, was very concerned and was questioning him. *"Who is the Prime Minister of Canada?" "What day of the month is it?" "What day of the week is it?"* Neil answered every question correctly.

I told the doctor, *"Ask him what day it is the day after tomorrow."* That would be December 23, my birthday. Neil thought for a moment, and answered, *"That's Ruth's birthday."*

The doctor wasn't convinced though, and expressed concern about possible internal bleeding.

The enemy's final round

After some time, the doctor finally responded, *"Well, you are going to have a nasty headache for a few days."* Neil had been supernaturally healed of 40 years of migraine headaches not that long before this happened. They had controlled our lives, striking at inopportune times, cancelling family outings, and disrupting plans. Being a gentle person, his quiet response was *"No."*

The doctor disagreed. *"Yes, you will!"*

Recognizing that the enemy was trying to find an opening to put the headaches back on him, he spoke with a little more authority. *"No, I won't!"* Again the doctor said, *"Yes, you will!"*

At this point, Neil sat up suddenly and with a wave of his hand, declared with finality, *"No, I won't have a headache. I'm through with headaches!"*

Surprised at the unexpected outburst, the doctor conceded quietly, *"Well, maybe you won't."* And he didn't!

At the time of this writing, it's been twenty-six years since he was delivered and he hasn't had a headache since that time! All glory to God! Our hearts go out to people who suffer with this terrible affliction. Our oldest daughter was healed of them at the same time as Neil. She had suffered with migraines since she was a toddler.

The doctor discharged him with final instructions. *"Stay off work for three days, don't drive any vehicles, and go home and rest."*

We went home and he rested for a bit, but it was useless because he was well! Before the day was out, he was back at the jobsite as if nothing had ever happened!

By the time I got the call from the hospital, I had diligently memorized Psalms 91 the way I had been instructed. It had become so real to me that I was *absolutely convinced* that it was God's will to provide protection to those who know the benefits included in our covenant with Him.

Obedience brings rewards

How very, very thankful I was that I had obeyed that very gentle impression of the Holy Spirit when He instructed me to memorize Psalms 91.

I was so glad I had not procrastinated or dismissed it. Not only did obedience prevent serious injury or death, but it taught me a valuable lesson in not only hearing the voice of God, but the importance of prompt obedience.

It would have been very easy to dismiss that still, small Voice, or just think that it was my imagination. Or I could have recognized it as God's Voice, but decided to put off the memorization until a later time.

Right or wrong thinking—life or death

There was a time in my life that I would have believed that the dream was a *premonition* of what was to come, the employee's comment about building Neil's coffin was the *confirmation*, and when the call came from the hospital, my response would have resulted in the *manifestation.*

I would have said, "*I just knew this would happen. First of all I had the dream, then the comment about the coffin, and now it's happened. It must be God's will.*" I would have come into total agreement with the enemy and his plan because of the picture he had painted. Many Christians lack the knowledge of God's will and His Word, and in this way allow the enemy to operate in their lives. I am so thankful that God is all-knowing and gave me instructions ahead of time so that He could make arrangements to prevent this tragedy.

> If everything that happens is God's will, why should we even bother to pray?

If you have experienced tremendous loss and tragedy, my heart is moved with compassion for you. My passion in life is to encourage people. If you have experienced blow after blow until you feel like the wind has been knocked out of you, then this book is for you! With everything in me, I desire to give you hope, to throw out a lifeline because I've been there. I know what it's like to lose hope, to feel like you're going down for the last time. But someone threw me a lifeline and pulled me to shore and resuscitated me with the Word! I long to do the same for you!

There may be things stolen from you that cannot be replaced this side of heaven, like the tragic death of a loved one. We know the pain of that too. However, the enemy can take advantage of us if we have a lack of knowledge in a certain area.[18] Religion teaches that God will take a loved one from us to teach us a lesson, or that He'll use sickness to train us. That's abuse! Any earthly father who would do that would be arrested and jailed, and rightfully so! John 10:10 is very clear—good God, bad devil.

> *The thief does not come except to steal, and to kill, and to destroy. I have come that they may have life, and that they may have it more abundantly.*
>
> (NKJV)

That's not difficult to understand — it's the devil that steals, kills and destroys. Jesus came to give us life; and not just ordinary life, but abundant life! As a matter of fact, He came to destroy the work of the devil![19]

So we must know where to put the blame when bad things happen. The Bible also says that the enemy is capable of killing only our physical body if he can, but not our spirit.

Let me tell you how the Lord made arrangements to prepare me for this attack. He knew that my lack of knowledge in this area could cause destruction. ***Please pay close attention, because this information could literally be a matter of life and death to you, as it was to us.***

> Experience is not the best teacher. That's a lie!

Although God is all-knowing and all-powerful, He can only intervene in our lives to the extent that we allow Him. He can warn us of impending events, but unless we are sensitive to His gentle nudges and act accordingly, His hands are tied. Unfortunately, often people don't heed and He gets the blame for what happens. People will respond by saying *"It must have been God's will,"* or *"God*

---

18 My people are destroyed for lack of knowledge. Hosea 4:6 KJV

19 For this purpose the Son of God was manifested, that He might destroy the works of the devil. I John 3:8b NKJV

is sovereign," or *"God allowed it to happen."* That is how I used to believe. To say that God is sovereign sounds very spiritual, but we must know what that means.

A sovereign head of state is one who is the ruling authority and his word is enforced as the final authority. God doesn't force His will on us—we can choose whether or not we want to be His subjects. God does not rule in the life of every person, not even in the life of every Christian! That kind of belief takes no faith whatsoever. If everything that happens is God's will, why should we even bother to pray? That kind of thinking makes humans little more than puppets. Or why should we seek medical help? If we believe God put a sickness on us to teach us a lesson, why would we see a doctor? Wouldn't that be contrary to God's will?

I heard a humorous commentary in regards to the belief that everything in life is predestined by God. A man fell down the stairs and broke his leg. His comment was, "Praise God, that's over with!"

> Don't misunderstand — bad things aren't always the result of disobedience. Sometimes we don't recognize the Holy Spirit's subtle warning of danger.

A parent can say to a child, *"I don't want you to play on the road."* Yes, the parent is "sovereign" in the sense that the child belongs to him, but he cannot force the child to obey. The child can choose to disobey and play on the roadway. Is it the fault of the parent if the child is injured or killed by not obeying? We wouldn't say, *"It must have been the parent's will because he allowed it to happen."* Of course, we would all agree that kind of thinking is absurd. Why would we attribute that kind of thinking to God?

Please don't misunderstand—bad things aren't always the result of disobedience. Sometimes it's the result of not recognizing the Holy Spirit's subtle warning of danger. We have experienced that, and learned the hard way several times. In each case, when we looked back, we could see where the Holy Spirit tried to get our attention to warn us, but we weren't sensitive enough to pick up on it. God always tries to show us things to come so that we are forewarned.

> *However, when He, the Spirit of truth, has come, He will guide you into all truth; for He will not speak on His own authority, but whatever He hears He will speak; and **He will tell you things to come.***
>
> John 16:13 NKJV (Emphasis mine)

Religion teaches that God puts sickness on us to teach us a lesson. Yet God is very clear in His Word about how earthly fathers should treat their children—He makes absolutely no allowance for a parent to abuse a child. How irrational it is to think that God would abuse His children by inflicting sickness or tragedy on them to teach them! That's twisted thinking. God is not the author of confusion.

> *For God is not the author of confusion but of peace.*
>
> I Cor. 14:33a NKJV

When you really think about it, would it be reasonable for God to give you a child, for example, and then kill that child in a few years? Wouldn't that be confusion and abuse? How could you trust a God like that?

The Bible is clear that God teaches us through His Word, by His Spirit, and by the five-fold ministry gifts He established to equip us.

> *And He Himself gave some to be apostles, some prophets, some evangelists, and some pastors and teachers, for the equipping of the saints for the work of ministry, for the edifying of the body of Christ.*
>
> Ephesians 4:11, 12 NKJV

Of course we can learn from the mistakes we make, but that is certainly not the best way to learn. Experience is *not* the best teacher! That's a lie. As a matter of fact, the Bible records the sins and mistakes of people so that we can learn from their mistakes and avoid doing the same things ourselves!

> *These things happened to them as examples for us. They were written down to warn us who live at the end of the age.*
>
> I Cor. 10:11 NLT

CHAPTER 5

Arrangements When Falsely Accused

Before I share my experience, I want to provide a bit of background. One of the things that really grieves me is to see people fall away from the Lord because of disappointment. Sometimes this happens when they experience betrayal by someone they trusted, or someone who should have stepped up to defend them but didn't.

A few years ago I was in our church service and my pastor made the comment *"Can't is out, and can is in!"* I jotted it down and thought to myself *"There's a poem in there."* As I put my thoughts on paper later on, I envisioned myself walking through a very old cemetery, something I actually enjoy doing. It's interesting to see the history, the family connections and the epitaphs on the tombstones.

But the cemetery I was walking through in my thoughts was not like that—there were no people buried there—only dreams. And there were tombstones as far as the eye could see. As I read the epitaphs on the marble headstones, I was shocked to find that they were all the same. What was the inscription? Simply two words—I CAN'T.

Can't is Out and Can is In

I wandered through a graveyard and read the epitaphs written there.
Not your ordinary graveyard, for only dreams were buried there.
It was an ancient cemetery, thousands of years old.
Each had the same inscription; "I CAN'T" etched in marble cold.

Underneath, in smaller letters, it described how the death occurred.
And almost without exception, the cause was a hurtful word.
Some were spoken by strangers who mocked their dream or plan.
Other words came from the mouth of a jealous woman or man.

Others from a loved one who belittled what was sacred to them.
So they buried their dream and inwardly vowed, "I'll never go there again."
I wept as I saw the gravestones, stretching for miles it seemed.
And I longed to unearth each treasure and revive each broken dream.

Then I heard the Voice of the Master, Who guards the dreams day and night.
"Whether you think you can or you can't, you're absolutely right!"
"For the human will is a gift from Me; only you can decide to quit.
So release those who have hindered you, and I'll give new life to it."

"Can't is out, and can is in," I clearly heard Him say.
"Death and life are in your tongue, so choose words of life today."
"Go back to the place where you left off, and decide to start anew.
Forgive yourself and others, and I'll make your dreams come true!"

When God asks someone to do something, it is often met with opposition. We shouldn't be surprised by that. The scriptures are full of examples of people who experienced great opposition and attack, yet they refused to give up. If they had, we most likely wouldn't even know about them.

People like Moses, Abraham, Joshua, Daniel, Esther, Ruth and many more. The very course of history depended on them. What if Ruth had gotten bitter after the death of her first husband and stayed in Moab? She was destined to be in the royal line from which Jesus would come, but she didn't know that.

And we don't know what's all at stake if we cool off spiritually and don't complete our assignments. God is arranging divine connections for you and for me! There are people we are called to impact. We've been called to be light and salt, but if we allow people or situations to cloud our lamp or lose our flavor, the destiny of many people can be affected.

One of the greatest tools in the enemy's arsenal is offense. No one is immune. The reason it's so effective is because it usually causes a chain reaction. When we get infected with offense, we pass it on to others, especially our loved ones. They get offended because they see our pain.

> Forgiveness is a spiritual force.

A bit later on, I will share with you the secret of how we got free of that trap and the amazing blessings that followed. It was one of the most difficult things we went through, but it's also one of the greatest life lessons that we learned. Forgiveness is a spiritual force.

> Sometimes God gives us a dream or plan or a piece of information and it's not for anyone else to know. It's given to us as a prayer assignment.

Let's look at the story of Joseph and the adversity he experienced. We can learn some things about the awesome power of forgiveness and focus, and the resulting blessing it brought not only to Joseph, but to future generations!

Joseph was his dad's favorite. That wasn't wise of his father, it wasn't fair either, but it happens. So many people have never gotten past a sibling being favored!

Joseph was just a lad of seventeen years when he had the dream about his brothers bowing down to him. **It's not always wise to share your dreams with everyone.** Sometimes God gives us a dream or plan or a piece of information but it's not for anyone else to know. It's given to us as a prayer assignment.

This was the case with Joseph's dream. It would be manifested many years later, but in his excitement about the dream, he alienated his brothers who were already resentful toward him. Unfortunately, this is how many of the dreams end up in the graveyard.

Many Christians have given up because they didn't see their dream become a reality. They buried the dream either because they got hurt, or it looked impossible or because someone made light of it.

Most often, your dream or assignment will be revealed in stages. God is into relationships and He wants you to stay connected to Him. Therefore, He will not reveal the whole plan at once. He will give it to you in stages so that you don't run ahead of yourself. It's like a puzzle; you may know the general picture, but not the fine details. Most often, if He showed us the whole plan at once, we would only see the difficulties and challenges involved, and pass it by.

When you are endeavoring to follow God, sometimes your siblings or parents will not understand and may even ridicule or persecute you. They may fail to recognize your gift. Jesus experienced this with His own family. The Bible says some of them thought He was crazy and out of His mind.

One time Jesus entered a house, and the crowds began to gather again. Soon he and his disciples couldn't even find time to eat. When his family heard what was happening, they tried to take him away. "He's out of his mind," they said.

Mark 3:20,21 NLT

Sometimes they will accuse you of thinking you are better than they. It's important to walk in humility. The Word says that if we humble ourselves under the mighty hand of God, He will EXALT us!

Your reaction to slander, false accusation and betrayal will determine your destiny and the destiny of others. Joseph's brothers stripped him of his distinctive garment. At times you may be stripped of your reputation by slander or false accusation. Your motives may be questioned, and you will be tempted to strike back. Don't do it! Rather, pray a blessing on your accuser and wait for God to come to your defense.

Years later, another one of Joseph's garments was stripped from him, with false accusations brought against him by Potiphar's wife. It's absolutely vital that we continue to make ourselves vulnerable once more rather than building up walls that we think will protect us. They will only imprison us.

> Your reaction to slander, false accusation and betrayal will determine your destiny and, as a result, the destiny of others.

Joseph didn't compromise his standards even though it cost him dearly. He was just a young man, single and very good looking with power and favor. He had no one of his faith with whom he could fellowship. His parents weren't there to hold him accountable or to nurture him. He didn't have a church to attend or a Bible to read. He could easily have thought *"I can do what I please. There's no one here that knows me. Besides, my family turned against me. If that's what God is like, I don't want anything to do with Him."* So many Christians have fallen into that snare. Things don't go right, and they blame God.

It may be that you have been loyally and faithfully serving someone and they believe a slanderous lie spread by a jealous individual, and the one who should know you best and come to your defense sides with the accuser. That can be devastating. That is what happened to me.

When those whom you have loyally served betray you or falsely accuse you, stay focused. It's not over till it's over. When Potiphar turned on Joseph and threw him into prison, Joseph wasn't even given a chance to tell his side of the story. Still, Joseph stayed positive; even in prison, Joseph got favor and promotion. Cream rises to the top, and you can't keep someone like that down!

The Lord was with Joseph and showed him mercy and lovingkindness and gave him favor in the sight of the warden of the prison. The warden committed to Joseph's care all the prisoners and whatsoever was done there, he was in charge of it. The warden paid no attention to anything that was in Joseph's charge, for the Lord was with him and made him prosper! God was making arrangements for Joseph!

When you are falsely accused, passed up for a promotion that should have been yours, fired unjustly, rejected by loved ones, get your eyes on the bigger picture.

If Joseph had gotten depressed and lost his focus, we would probably never have heard anything more about him. The prisons of our own making are full of people who got offended and parked at that spot, never to move on. God had a bigger plan for Joseph and He does for you too! That's why it's vitally important that you stay focused so that God can bless and promote you in order to fulfill your assignment.

Develop patience. Joseph spent 13 years in prison for a crime he didn't commit. No one came to his defense. He didn't get out early for good behavior. He had no rights; he was still a slave. But you wouldn't have known it by the way he carried himself.

Don't see yourself as a victim, but as a victor! If you get a victim mentality, you will never succeed.

Your gift will make room for you. Eventually the very thing that got Joseph into trouble ended up being what got him out of prison! He interpreted a dream. The Bible talks about not casting your pearls before the swine. Simply put, it means "don't put your pearls in the wrong place." Pearls don't belong in the mud or dirt. When Joseph shared his dream with his family as a youth, he was putting something sacred before those who would trample on it.

Eventually in prison, someone remembered that Joseph could interpret dreams and it came at a time when the king needed it. It also spared the head of the butler. But the butler soon forgot about his promise to Joseph and he spent another two years in prison. But then Pharaoh had a dream. Not Potiphar, but Pharaoh. This was the head guy! Then the butler remembered Joseph, who was hastily summoned out of prison. Because Joseph didn't get offended, his gift wasn't buried in the graveyard; rather, God was able to use it to save lives!

Act as though you already have your breakthrough! Joseph had class. Yes, he wanted to get out of prison, but he first shaved, changed his clothes and made himself presentable before appearing before Pharaoh. Joseph just knew he was destined for great things and he acted in a manner that was fitting for greatness.

One of the ways to keep from getting offended is to put on the garment of praise and dress for spiritual success. We need to have on the whole armor of God. The breastplate of integrity is part of that armor.

Joseph not only had the interpretation; he had the solution. Remember, you have the Spirit of Wisdom abiding in you and He will teach you all things. Be aware of the fact that the Holy Spirit sees your situation from every angle; that's why we need to stay in close communication with Him. You are gifted to solve someone's problem. It can be the door to your promotion.

Lawyers solve legal problems, mechanics solve mechanical problems, and dentists solve tooth problems and so on. In the same way that every cell of our body has an assignment, we are a "cell" in the body of Christ and have an assignment to fulfill our destiny. We must not bury it in the graveyard.

Joseph went from the prison to the palace in a day! God is making arrangements for your breakthrough too! What if Joseph had given up after the first year? Expect the "suddenlies" of God on your behalf and others. Make happen for someone else what you would like to happen for you.

Your breakthrough is also for someone else! Joseph's attitude and subsequent promotion saved a nation from famine. But even more than that, it saved his own family from starvation and brought about restoration and healing to those who had mistreated him so badly. He repaid evil with good. That's an example of maturity and grace, and that's what will happen if we operate in forgiveness and blessing toward those who have hurt us.

I would venture to say there are thousands upon thousands of people who stepped out of their service for the Lord because someone hurt them. Many have suffered spiritual abuse and have walked away from the Lord, but countless others who still love God no longer attend church or trust any spiritual leaders or fellow Christians. They will never advance to the potential that God has in mind for them until they allow God to resurrect them and learn to trust again. Until then, their gift lies buried in that graveyard.

Earlier I told you that I would share with you a lesson that Neil and I learned about the power of forgiveness and how we made it a practice to bless those who falsely accused and slandered us.

I have chosen not to provide all the details because doing so would identify certain people involved; we have forgiven them and blessed them and have been reconciled with all but one person.

Because of a position I held at the time, the enemy used an individual to turn a large group of people against me in hopes that I would lose the position. I was not immediately aware of it until this group went to my employer who was a Christian. I was not told what the accusations were nor was I told who my accusers were. Never being given an opportunity to scripturally confront my accusers, and having been a faithful employee for many years, this was a blow I had not expected. We felt alone and abandoned. At the same time, we were experiencing tremendous financial challenges. However, because I kept my heart right, God made arrangements to vindicate me.

We knew it was really the enemy behind this attack, but it was very difficult to lose so many friends. Only one couple believed in us.

The heartache was almost unbearable but we were determined to do the Word. We had been through hard times before and the Lord always delivered us, so we were determined more than ever to take the high road and survive. We were not looking for a way to get blessed; we were looking for a way to get through this attack and still love God. It had nothing to do with trying to keep my position. I would gladly have resigned if I had felt God's leading in that direction. Furthermore, we didn't tell our children what was happening because we didn't want them to take offense on our behalf. We knew that giving in to offense would destroy us and affect our children. It was too great a price to pay.

Please pay very careful attention, because this will be a major key in your victory!

It was at this time that we discovered the wealth in Luke chapter 6 in the Amplified Bible.

> *27 But I say to you who are listening now to Me: [in order to heed, make it a practice to] love your enemies, treat well (do good to, act nobly toward) those who detest you and pursue you with hatred,*

We knew that love is not a feeling—it's a choice, so we chose to pray blessings on them throughout the day. We printed Luke 6 and posted it in places where we would continually see it. I carried it my purse to study when I had a minute or two.

This verse talks about heeding—to lean over to listen carefully and to make it a practice, so that's exactly what we did. But it didn't stop at just commanding us to love them and treat them well. It went a step further!

> *28 Invoke blessings upon and pray for the happiness of those who curse you, implore God's blessing (favor) upon those who abuse you [who revile, reproach, disparage, and high-handedly misuse you]. 31 And as you would like and desire that men would do to you, do exactly so to them.*

Invoke and implore are strong words! To invoke means to call on God to bless them, to appeal to God to bless them, to summon God to bless them, and to implore means to invoke with tears!

In other words, I must use the same intensity in praying for their blessing as I would want for myself! So that's what we did. And because we knew so many of them intimately, we knew what they needed, so it was easy to know what to pray.

> *35 But love your enemies and be kind and do good [doing favors so that someone derives benefit from them] and lend, expecting and hoping for nothing in return but considering nothing as lost and despairing of no one; and then your recompense **(your reward) will be great (rich, strong, intense, and abundant)**, and you will be sons of the Most High, for He is kind and charitable and good to the ungrateful and the selfish and wicked.*
>
>   (Emphasis mine)

I couldn't help notice the promise of a reward so great that it's described as intense—red hot! Even though that's not why we were doing this, we saw that it came with a reward and that when we did these things, we would be pleasing our Father.

> *36 So be merciful (sympathetic, tender, responsive, and compassionate) even as your Father is [all these].*

> *37 Judge not [neither pronouncing judgment nor subjecting to censure], and you will not be judged; do not condemn and pronounce guilty, and you will not be condemned and pronounced guilty;* ***acquit and forgive and release (give up resentment, let it drop),*** *and you will be acquitted and forgiven and released.*

So we decided we wouldn't judge them guilty, but we would leave that in God's hands. We would acquit them and bless them as if this had never happened.

> *47 For everyone who comes to Me and listens to My words [in order to heed their teaching] and does them,* ***I will show you what he is like:***

> *48 He is like a man building a house, who dug and went down deep and laid a foundation upon the rock; and when a flood arose, the torrent broke against that house and could not shake or move it, because it had been securely built or founded on a rock.*

> (Emphasis mine)

These two scriptures were especially meaningful because we didn't only want to get through this challenge, but we wanted to become spiritually stable and unmovable as a result of heeding these scriptures. That meant not only hearing it but doing it!

I also discovered a verse that I thought must surely be a misprint.

> *So if you are presenting a sacrifice at the altar in the Temple and you suddenly remember that someone* ***has something against you,*** *leave your sacrifice there at the altar. Go and be reconciled to that person. Then come and offer your sacrifice to God.*

> Matthew 5:23, 24 NLT (Emphasis mine)

I had always thought it said "if *you* have something against someone."

We had been applying these scriptures for some time and it really helped us not to sink into emotional despair. Being shunned by those who used to be close friends was not easy. It was always in our face.

I thank God for a spiritually strong husband and we kept each other accountable and encouraged each other.

I so clearly recall what happened one morning as I was having my quiet time in the Boardroom of my office before opening time. I had read the Word and then turned off the light to sit in the dark to hear from God without distractions. I had been praying for the people involved, blessing them, praying for their children, their businesses, their finances, etc. Up to this time, I had been praying by faith, not by feelings.

You see, feelings are like the caboose on a train that follows along where the engine is going. The Word was my engine and my feelings were the caboose.

Suddenly it was as if the glory of the Lord filled the room and I felt an overwhelming love for these people that is difficult to describe. I felt as if I were glowing. I felt such an intense desire for them to be blessed that I could hardly contain myself.

I could sense God's power so strongly and in my joy I said to God, *"Lord, I'm asking You to surprise them! I wish I could peek in the window and see their joy when you surprise them."*

Remember, I was still sitting in the dark, but down in my spirit, I heard this: *"You will travel around the world."*

My immediate reaction was that my mind had strayed because I hadn't even been praying about that. There were far too many other pressing things to pray about, and we were just focusing on getting through this situation. But the Holy Spirit was helping me, so I just said *"I receive that!"*

I finished my devotions and went to my office to begin the day. A short while later, Neil stopped by. He stood in the doorway and with great reverence asked, *"What's happening here?"* He could tell, without my saying a word that something had happened! It was the glory of God.

I never mentioned about the travel. It wasn't my focus. We just rejoiced in the presence of God.

Later that evening, the phone rang and someone I hardly knew was calling from another province to ask if Neil and I would like to accompany them on a trip to Israel, all expenses paid! To say I was shocked would be an understatement. They needed an answer by the next day, so I explained that I would talk to Neil as soon as he got home, and I would call them back.

When I hung up, I went to our bedroom and threw myself across the bed, still shaking. I had forgotten about the word that morning in regards to travelling the world. I said to the Lord, *"How come You did that when I didn't even ask for that?"* The words were hardly out of my mouth. His immediate response which blesses me to this day was, *"I wanted to surprise you!"* He used the very words that I had used when I prayed for my accusers that morning.

Well, we went on that wonderful trip and became good friends. I was home from Israel for 11 days when I received a trip to Switzerland. While on that trip, I was the recipient of a shopping spree and received a complete new wardrobe!

Since that time, I've been to Israel a second time, to Switzerland three times, to Hungary and Romania twice, and I've lost track of the number of times we've been to Hawaii and other places in the United States. I have literally travelled around the world, and God has paid for every trip, and not always by using the same people. In fact, we've been able to give trips to other people as well. And it all came about by blessing those who hurt us.

The wonderful thing is that forgiveness frees us. And that was just the start. It would take another book to share all the breakthroughs we have had in our family since we learned the power of forgiveness and blessing our enemies.

We were able to unearth those dreams that we had painfully buried—that we thought were forever gone. And like I always say, other people's victories depend on ours. If we had stayed in offense, our children would have suffered and so would future generations of our family line. Perhaps we wouldn't even be attending church today. We certainly wouldn't be walking in any degree of victory.

I've said all that to encourage you to walk out of that graveyard of offense and broken dreams. Make your way onto the highway of blessing and God's favor and fulfill the calling for which you were placed on this earth! It's not too late.

As I said earlier, through God making arrangements, we have been reconciled with everyone except for one couple. But here's a neat way that God made arrangements. Remember I mentioned that there was one couple who had believed in us? Well, they were friends with the "un-reconciled" couple. Through them we heard that the couple was facing some challenges. The husband had to undergo unexpected surgery and was unable to work for some time. God really put it on our heart to help them financially but they had made it clear they wanted absolutely no contact from us. So we prayed for God to make arrangements and show us how we could bless them, and He did!

We asked God to show us a figure that would cover their monthly mortgage payment. We shared it with the couple who believed in us and found that they would be seeing them shortly in another province. So we asked them if they would be willing to hand deliver the money anonymously, and of course, they were thrilled!

So we purchased brand new bills and put them in an envelope. We instructed them that if the couple asked who it was from, just tell them *"It's from someone who loves you!"*

Later they shared how it had played out. They took the couple out for supper. The husband was still recovering from surgery.

Our friends handed them the envelope across the table. As they opened it and saw the number of bills, their eyes grew wider and wider. Then they asked, *"Who is this from?"* They replied, *"From someone who loves you!"* The wife's response was *"Well, tell them we love them too!"*

So that's the final word on it! Even though we haven't been reconciled, we love each other!

I should add that my employer eventually saw the truth and approved of the way we had conducted ourselves during this challenge.

CHAPTER 6

Arrangements To Find a Spouse!

Over the years, God has often used me in the area of praying for a spouse for others. It's an area where my faith is strong. Towards the end of the chapter, I'll share some of those testimonies with you.

My husband, Neil, and I have been happily married since September 26, 1964. How God brought us together is a great example of how God made arrangements.

I recall praying for my future spouse as a child—I know that I was under the age of ten when I did this. I remember walking among the trees and talking to God out loud about a lot of things. One of those things was my future husband. I asked Him to give me a husband who would really love God and really love me.

That's not the usual kind of thing that children pray about, I don't think. I didn't pray about it every day or even every month. I just remember that I brought it up in prayer. Amazingly, I found out later that my future husband prayed the same childhood prayer! God was making the necessary arrangements in answer to our prayers.

I was a shy child, the twelfth in a family of fifteen children. My father was a pastor until I was ten, at which time he left the ministry. I didn't have an accurate picture of God—I thought He was watching my every move, waiting to "get me" if I stepped out of line. Yet I loved Him with all my heart.

In spite of the large family, our home was given to hospitality. That is how I first came to see a person with a different color of skin. I'll never forget that first impression. Mr. Thomas was a missionary from India. He was tall, with a head of thick, pure white hair, very white teeth and a huge smile. Because of my family's involvement in ministry, I developed a love for the ministry and for people in different parts of the world. My little world expanded, and so did my heart.

From my earliest memory, I wanted to do whatever I could to serve God. I can still see myself as a child of eight, among the trees on the farm, preaching. I saw myself doing that in the future. And it has come to pass.

God had gifted me musically, and I played a 12 bass accordion at the age of eight. My father was a circuit preacher and, on occasion, he took me along with him to play for the congregation. Or sometimes I would play a "special" on the church's pump organ (that really dates me!) although I could barely reach the pedals.

I had no formal musical training, but I so loved music that I just taught myself to play. I had no idea that God was making arrangements for me in that area as well! Later on in life, when our children were young, I was part of a Southern gospel quartet for 14 years. We traveled on weekends, made three recordings, and ministered in various parts of Saskatchewan, Manitoba and Alberta.

When we made our first recording, it was played a great deal on *Nitewatch*, a radio program hosted by a man we knew only as "Brother John."[20] It was through this man and his wife that we learned about the baptism with the Holy Spirit that changed our lives forever.

---

20 This program can still be heard on week nights on CKSW 570 in Saskatchewan. It celebrated 40 years in 2014.

But that's another story. Back to how I met my husband, Neil.

Although our families did not know each other, we grew up within twenty miles of each other. But back then, that was a long distance!

Like I said, I was quite shy and in high school I was a wallflower. My two closest friends were knockout beauties and very popular. I dated a couple of guys in high school, but not for any length of time and they certainly weren't serious relationships.

> I was unaware of the fact that God was making arrangements for me to meet my future spouse.

When I was sixteen years old, a family visited our home. They had an older teenage son who was very handsome. All the girls wanted to date him, but for some reason, he wanted to date me. Of course, I was flattered. My parents didn't allow it, and although I was upset, I obeyed. I found out later that his motives were not pure.

Being a parent and grandparent myself, I now know that God anoints parents to see potential pitfalls in order to protect their children, but at that time I was unaware of the fact that God was making arrangements for me to meet my future spouse. If I had been disobedient, I would have taken a completely different path, and only God knows what direction my life would have taken. I may never have met the man of my dreams.

That reminds me of a favorite scripture that I have shared often.

> *He who heeds instruction and correction is [not only himself] in the way of life [but also] is a way of life for others. And he who neglects or refuses reproof [not only himself] goes astray [but also] causes to err and is a path toward ruin for others.*
>
> Proverbs 10:17 Amplified Bible

If I had not heeded the instruction of my parents, I would have gone astray. This would have affected future generations. We need to be very conscious of the fact that other people's victory is dependent on ours!

It was only a few months later that I met Neil. Let me share with you the most unusual way God made arrangements for this to take place. In order to show you how miraculous it was, I must share something that happened to me when I was a toddler.

I have a twin brother, and no, we're not identical! It's hilarious how many people ask that. Two heads are better than one, they say, and the two of us could get into our share of mischief when we were little. On one occasion my parents were away and our older siblings were caring for the younger children. I don't remember the incident because I was too young, but it has been told to me.

We lived on the farm and my father kept a container of kerosene behind the porch door. Somehow I was able to open it and thinking it was juice, I drank it. When it was discovered, my older siblings tried to make me vomit by making me drink melted butter and swinging me around repeatedly, but all to no avail. I just wanted to sleep. I was rushed to the nearest hospital by tractor, four miles away! My parents had the car, so the tractor was the only option.

My oldest sister, who was on duty at the hospital, knew something was seriously wrong, for she was not allowed in the room.

Word spread quickly in the community and the surrounding towns about the little girl who was very sick. Twenty miles away, a father came home from town and told his family about the little girl who drank kerosene. His young son was so concerned for her and prayed for her to recover. Little did he know he was praying for his future wife!

So how did God bring us together? As a young man, Neil was planning to move from Saskatchewan to Alberta, and the church youth group was sorry to see him go. Having experienced a broken heart a year earlier, dating was not on his agenda. He was a godly young man, gentle and kind. The pastor's daughter asked him if he would agree to a blind date scheduled for the evening before he was moving to Red Deer, Alberta. He agreed.

And that's how God made arrangements for us to meet. I knew in my heart that he was the one the first night we met on September 11, 1962. Not only was he very handsome, but he had a well-known reputation as someone of high standards. I am so thankful to this day that I didn't miss out by choosing the wrong path. We were married two years later on September 26, 1964.

At the beginning of the chapter, I told you I would share several testimonies with you of how God allowed me to be a part of helping others believe for a spouse.

It's easy to apply faith in an area where you have experienced powerful answers to prayer. I know the blessing that a wonderful marriage relationship brings; therefore, I long to see others to experience it too.

My first assignment

I recall the first time it happened. I was shopping at a local mall and happened to meet a young lady whom I had known for many years. We hadn't seen each other for a few years, and by this time we had been married about twenty years.

After casual conversation in which I discovered she had a successful career in the medical field, I asked her how she was *really* doing. Normally, I would never have worded it that way, but I believe God was using that to make arrangements for her!

As soon as the words left my mouth, I noticed tears well up in her eyes. I took her hand and apologized and asked her if there was something I could pray about on her behalf. She shared with me that she longed to marry but had never even had one date. She was quite emotional so I asked her if we could get together to talk. I assured her that it was God's will for her to have a husband, and that He actually put that desire in her heart!

Shortly thereafter, she visited me at our home. She was a Christian, so when I showed her a few scriptures to confirm that God would grant her desire, it wasn't difficult to convince her. She just needed someone to come into agreement with her and give her hope. We prayed together and I could tell that the load was lifted. She was so grateful and asked what she could do for me in return. My reply was, *"Just send me a wedding invitation."* I received that invitation within a year!

If you're in that situation, let me share the scriptures that I shared with her.

> *Then the Lord God said, "It is not good for the man to be alone. I will make a helper who is just right for him."*
> Genesis 2:18 NLT

> *And we are confident that he hears us whenever we ask for anything that pleases him. And since we know he hears us when we make our requests, we also know that he will give us what we ask for.*
> I John 5:14, 15 NLT

Here are a few that I've discovered since then that show the value God places on you if you are desiring to be a godly wife. You are a gift from God! And the same applies to anyone desiring a spouse.

> *The man who finds a wife finds a treasure, and he receives favor from the LORD.*
> Proverbs 18:22 NLT

> *Fathers can give their sons an inheritance of houses and wealth, but only the LORD can give an understanding wife.*
> Proverbs 19:14 NLT

A capable, intelligent, and virtuous woman—who is he who can find her? She is far more precious than jewels and her value is far above rubies or pearls.

Proverbs 31:10 Amplified

My second assignment

Shortly thereafter, Neil and I were guests on a TV program around the Easter season. Towards the end of the program, I felt I had a word from the Lord for someone who was watching the program. The host encouraged me to share it.

This is what it was. *"There's someone watching the program to-day and you are very discouraged. Your dreams are in the tomb, but God wants you to know that He wants to resurrect those dreams. You have believed for a husband but he hasn't come. Other people have thrown cold water on your dreams, telling you it's impossible. But the things that are impossible with man are possible with God."*

I encouraged that person to call in for prayer. The show was taped on Saturday and aired Sunday morning.

Sunday afternoon I received a call from the prayer co-ordinator saying that a young lady had called after watching the program, saying she was that person I had been talking about, and that she'd like to talk to me. She said she knew me, so I was asked if I'd like to call her.

It turns out that I did know her in the past but hadn't seen her for several years. This young lady had a physical handicap from birth and had never dated. Someone had taken advantage of her vulnerability, resulting in pregnancy and the subsequent birth of a precious son. At the time the program aired, her son was old enough to understand that he didn't have a father. Together, the two of them had been praying for a husband and father. Well-meaning people told her not to build her son's hopes; after all, who would marry a handicapped girl with a child?

I encouraged her to take the word that I had shared on the program, as if it came not from me, but from the Lord. And I told her that her son's prayers were vital, for children pray in faith! I also suggested that it's not wise to tell just anyone about what you believe God to do, especially if they will try to talk you out of it. It's like "casting your pearls before the swine."[21] That scripture used to bother me because I don't like to refer to people as pigs. Then I got further understanding of what this verse really means. It is really saying that you shouldn't put something precious in the wrong place. Pearls don't belong in the pigpen, and you shouldn't put your dreams in a place where they'll be trampled.

After we had prayed, she was so tremendously encouraged and determined that she would not let go of her dream again.

I asked her to send me a wedding invitation, which I received within the year!

My third assignment

Several years ago I became acquainted with a woman who moved to Canada. She had gone through some unfortunate circumstances and was emotionally and spiritually wounded. I met her for coffee and listened as she shared her story. Divorced years earlier, she had raised her children, who were now adults. She admired the relationship that my husband and I share and spoke longingly of her desire to have that kind of marriage. I shared with her how God had used me in that area several times and emphasized that it was God's will to give her the desire of her heart. She agreed that it was definitely her desire.

I encouraged her to go home and make a "list" of what she desired in a spouse, and write down several corresponding scriptures as a foundation for prayer. Then we would meet again and pray in agreement for her prayer to be answered.

---

21 "Do not give what is holy to the dogs; nor cast your pearls before swine."
   Matthew 7:6a NKJV

A short while later we met and she showed me her "list." She wanted someone who had a good relationship with God, who would love her and her family as his own and who would have the same vision for ministry. She expressed the desire for her spouse to be considerate, strong yet gentle, and that they would complete each other. He would be strong in areas where she was weak, and vice versa.

We prayed over the list before we parted, and she gave me the list. She was committed to do her part and leave the arrangements to God. In the meantime, she would concentrate on allowing God to restore and heal her.

For the time being she was staying with a friend but needed to find more permanent living arrangements. In the meantime, her brother and sister-in-law moved to the city to attend school and found temporary rental accommodations for the school year. They encouraged her to move there too so they could spend more time together.

It was a large home with many bedrooms, owned by a retired Christian man who was single. He had decided to rent rooms to Christian students and give them the run of the house, so to speak.

He had also been divorced and raised a son who was now an adult. Being a very personable fellow, he was glad to have people around him and enjoyed spending evenings with his tenants, visiting and getting to know them.

Someone had once asked him if he would ever remarry. His reply was, *"God would have to bring her to my door!"* It took him a while to realize that God had done just that!

They were married approximately a year later and at their wedding, I took out the list she had given me and read it for all to hear. Everyone was amazed at how God answered her prayer to the smallest detail.

Spouses for our children

Because Neil and I had seen the way God answered our child-hood prayers for each other, it was only natural that we prayed for the future spouse of each of our three children. We did this while they were still in my womb. Neil often placed his hands on our unborn children and prayed for them, for God to direct their lives and bring them the right spouse.

Our oldest child married the boy next door. Our families attended the same church, and the two of them started first grade together and graduated high school together. She had many opportunities to date others, but her response was *"I know I'm going to marry Trevor so why should I lead anyone else on?"* Many of their dates were on the front steps of our homes.

They graduated from Rhema Bible Training College in Tulsa, Oklahoma in 1999 and have been pastors of Calgary Word of Faith Church in Calgary, Alberta, for nearly 14 years at the time of this writing.

And God has so wonderfully answered all those prayers. We are so blessed to have two sons-in-law who are as dear to us as our son.

It amazes me to see how God has equipped each of our children and their spouses. My husband and I made so many mistakes in raising our children and wished we had done many things differently. Their parenting skills surpass ours by a country mile. We are so grateful to the Lord for this.

My faith was growing in the area of praying for people for a spouse, so I thought I may as well pray in a wife for our only son who was about to turn thirty years old.

He was very popular and had many "girl" friends, but no "girlfriend." He had experienced a broken heart in his late teens and determined he would never date again until God showed him the right girl.

One by one his buddies were getting married and starting families. One day he and I were driving somewhere and I asked him if he had a "shopping list" of what he'd like in a wife. I told him to get a picture in his mind of what she's like so that when she comes into view, he would know it's her.

"What do you mean?" he said. I replied, *"Be specific. Tell God what you like; for example, what hair colour do you prefer? Do you want her tall or short? What personality type do you envision?"*

As we talked, we gained a visual picture of what his future wife would be like.

She would be someone who would be committed to God. She would be his height, slim, and have long hair, in a darker shade. She would have a good sense of humour and fit in well with our family, as he would with hers. She would enjoy outdoor activities and be physically fit.

I began to pray for this girl and thank God that she was coming on the scene.

They were married about a year later on March 4, 2001 and she fits the profile perfectly. She has dubbed me her "mother-in-love," and I'm blessed to also be her friend.

That left our youngest daughter. She met her husband-to-be when they both attended Bible School. He's a helicopter pilot who decided to take a year off to go to Bible school. We can see how God made the arrangements. He's a wonderful husband and provider and fits in so well in our family.

We have been blessed with eight wonderful grandchildren, and we began praying for *their* spouses even before they were born.

So I encourage you to paint the canvas of your future in prayer. God has already been in your future and He wants you to get involved in it! He needs your participation.

A word of exhortation

I have had occasions where someone asked me to pray for them for a spouse, having heard of some of these testimonies.

I recall one such occasion. A pastor friend had told her about me and encouraged her to see me.

Let me be clear. It is God that answers prayer. I simply come into agreement with the person by faith. I give Him all the credit for anything He does through me or for me.

So I explained to her that she should seek God for what she wanted in a husband and to write it down and get scriptures to stand on.

When she brought the list to me, I was somewhat taken aback. At the top of her list was "nice buns." Needless to say, there was no point in pursuing it any further. Such flippancy[22] in dealing with a matter of choosing a life's partner shows a lack of respect for God and the institution of marriage that He created for our benefit and enjoyment.

Beware of counterfeits

Even though God is making arrangements in response to your prayer, there is an enemy out there who will try to get you off track. He hates successful marriages. If he can't get you to doubt God, he'll try to introduce a counterfeit.

This is where you need to stay on guard and protect yourself against deception.

I know of several instances where I stood in prayer with someone for a spouse. They did so well for a time and then suddenly fell for someone who showed interest in them, but didn't line up with the qualifications they had laid out.

---

22 "Don't be flip with the sacred. Banter and silliness give no honor to God." Matthew 7:6 The Message

In each case the marriage was not the blessing it could have been if they had waited for God's best.

Just because you meet someone who is interested in you, or someone you are attracted to, does not mean it's the one God is arranging for you! This is where you need to stay on guard and protect yourself against deception. During this time, you will be tempted to let your emotions rule you. I can't stress strongly enough how you must guard yourself at this most vulnerable time. Remember, God will send you the best and you'll be glad you waited!

There is a belief so popular today that "every person who comes into your life is sent by God for a reason." This has led so many people into error. The enemy can come as an angel of light and send not only counterfeits, but people who are assigned to drain you of energy, time and resources.

CHAPTER 7

Arrangements to Recover Stolen Property

It was the summer of 1996 and I was planning to meet a colleague for lunch. A sickening feeling came over me as it slowly dawned on me that my purse was missing! It not only contained my personal ID and effects, but the church offering which needed to be counted and deposited. Thankfully, most of it was made up of cheques.

> I asked God to put an honest person in contact with my purse and that the angels would watch over it.

It also contained my credit cards, the keys to my car, office and home, along with the address of our home! As well, there were pictures of my children and grandchildren, some pieces of jewelry and other personal items. Everything except the kitchen sink—it was a large organizer purse. Unknown to me at the time, there was a whole lot more missing than my purse. This would turn out to be a most unusual story!

It was noon by the time I noticed my purse was missing. The thief could have taken it three hours ago! I mentally retraced my steps a hundred times since arriving at my office that morning. Could I have forgotten it at the gas station? I was so sure I had set it on my desk. Oh yes, I realized, I definitely had it when I arrived at work that morning, because it held the keys to unlock the church. By now the thief could have robbed our home!

It was my custom to start the day with reading the scriptures and praying for the needs of the ministry for which I worked. Shortly thereafter, the church secretary summoned me to her office adjacent to mine, where I spent 20 minutes helping her with a computer problem.

Staking my claim

After the initial shock had worn off, I called the Saskatoon City Police. Then I declared to the pastor and secretary, *"I call back my purse in Jesus' Name. I ask that an honest person come into contact with my purse, and I post the angels of God to watch over it."*

In the meantime, there were details to see to. After notifying the police, I called a locksmith to have a key made for my car. I cancelled my credit cards, called the bank, and prayed for angels to watch over our home.

You'll never see your purse again!

The police came to take my report and said that the thief had probably thrown the purse into one of the many dumpsters in the area. The church was located in a light industrial area with many businesses and mini-malls in the area, all of which had dumpsters. They were kind enough to comb the immediate area and searched the dumpsters for any sign of my purse.

Later in the day, they called me to say, *"Ma'am, I'm afraid you'll never see your purse again. These dumpsters are emptied every few days and there's no telling where it could be. We've searched those in the area and there's no sign of it."* I thanked them, but when I hung up I said, *"That's their report, but my report is that it will come back to me."*

I just need money for baby food and diapers

The evening before the theft occurred, several of us had been working late at the church. A young man came to the door and asked my husband for money—just enough for baby food and diapers. Neil asked him to wait by the door while he went to get me, as I was the church administrator.

Churches are often the targets of scams, and my first response was *"That sounds like a con."* Almost immediately I repented of my judgmental attitude and followed my husband to the front door. But the man wasn't there! It was already dark and we were unable to see where he had gone. My husband described him as short, with a small build, reddish hair and freckles.

Looking back, I believe he hid inside the building that night and easily left unnoticed the next morning. If he had entered the church that morning, we would have heard the door open, as it was right next to the office. I gave the man's description to the police.

> My first thought was, "That sounds like a con."

Later that day, I went next door to pay the rent and told the landlord what had happened to us. She informed me that someone matching that description had also come to their door the night before, bleeding from his arm, asking for a towel. She went to the restroom to get it, and returned to find the man gone and her purse missing!

Meanwhile, the police were receiving numerous reports from the area of someone matching the same description asking for money for "baby food and diapers." In each case, a purse was missing!

The pastor of another church in the same vicinity reported that a man fitting the description also asked for money for baby food and diapers but did not gain entrance to their building.

All of this just toughened my resolve to have my items returned and see this man brought to justice. At least half a dozen businesses had been robbed and many of the employees greatly inconvenienced by this "con man." If he was indeed the man responsible for the theft, I had been right about my "first impression!" Not a very comforting thought at that point.

Cast not away your confidence

> Our imaginations were intended to be a screen to preview coming attractions!

I made up my mind that from the day of the theft until the return of my property, I was going to hang on to what I had declared and not let go of it. I thanked God continually that the angels were watching over my property and an honest person was going to come in contact with it. I refused to waver. I imagined getting the call that my belongings were found. This helped me believe.

God created our imagination. It is something good, not evil. Our imaginations were intended to be a screen to preview coming attractions! Just like anything that God created, it can be perverted and used for evil if our motives are wrong. If given permission, the enemy uses it to preview coming failures, and unfortunately, we often receive those previews as truth.

When God told Abram to look at the stars in the sky, He wanted him to get a picture of how numerous his descendants would be. God did that for a reason—so Abram would be able to "see" or imagine it! God designed us in such a way that words paint pictures.

For example, if I say "purple three-legged dog," you immediately visualize it. That's not wrong! God made us that way; that's why we need to be careful what we hear, because the Word says, "faith comes by hearing." Faith is trust, and when we trust something, we believe it. It's important to know that what we believe or trust is truth, or we will be deceived.

When you worry, you get the thought, your mind imagines it, and the feelings reinforce it.

When the enemy whispers thoughts of fear, failure or tragedy and you entertain it, you are simply "trusting" that he's telling you the truth. Then the accompanying emotions kick in and you actually "feel" it, and you can see it because you're imagining it! You have come into agreement with him. It's only a matter of time before you verbalize it. That is a description of worry. You get the thought, your mind imagines it, and the feelings reinforce it. Next you talk about it.

Let me give you an example of this from my own life. Before I had understanding of these things, I used to say, *"I get one good bout of the flu each winter, and then I'm done with it."* Guess what I got every winter? Exactly what I believed I would get. I created it with the words I believed and spoke.

If, on the other hand, we respond with "trust" in God's Word, fear goes out the door and confidence comes in—not just self confidence, but confidence in God and His ability to keep His Word.

Everything is small to a big God.

But back to my purse. With each passing day, people were telling me to forget about seeing my purse again. In the natural it didn't look hopeful, but I was not looking in the natural. My confidence was in God who could provide tax money in the mouth of a fish and feed 5,000 with a few small loaves and fishes. Everything is small to a big God—nothing is large to Him. Healing a cold or cancer is all small to Him, and I was confident that He knew exactly where my purse was.

An honest person finds my purse!

Approximately two weeks after the theft, I received an early morning call from a waitress in a downtown café. *"Are you Ruth Hamm?"* she asked. I told her yes. *"I just found your Bible in the dumpster."* My Bible? I hadn't even realized it was missing. I had so many Bibles in my office, and I read from different versions, so I had not noticed that one was missing! I told her that my purse had been stolen. She replied, *"There are a bunch of purses in the dumpster. If you can come down here with someone who can crawl in there, I will watch that no one touches anything until you get here!"*

Within minutes we were on our way—Neil outfitted with coveralls suitable for climbing into a restaurant dumpster! My joy knew no bounds—not just because it appeared my purse had been found, but because God had done exactly what I had asked! He put an honest person in contact with my property!

When we got there, we were amazed! There were seven purses, numerous Bibles, books and Sunday School materials, not only from our church, but other churches in the community. Moreover, this restaurant was miles from my office.

What are the chances of a thief dumping them in that location two weeks later, miles from where they were taken? What prevented him from putting them all in a garbage bag where they would never have been seen? What caused him to put them in that particular dumpster? The answer is easy! I had prayed that the angels would watch over my purse and cause an honest person to come in contact with it. That's exactly what happened! But that's not the end of the story! More surprises were in store!

Someone else's victory depends on yours

Not only did the answer to my prayer bring joy to me, but also to the other six people who were missing their purses! This reminds me of Proverbs 10:17a in the Amplified Bible.

He who heeds instruction and correction is [not only himself] in the way of life [but also] is a way of life for others.

When I looked through my purse, the only thing missing was the cash, amounting to $260.00, my health card and my blank cheques. Everything else was there—the cheques from the offering, and even my credit cards! I chuckled when I noticed he had even stolen a book I was reading, *How to Realize Your Full Potential.* Apparently, he hadn't taken time to read it, or maybe he had, and that's why it took two weeks!

We got a large garbage bag and put all the items in it and took them to the police station. They were quite amazed.

Don't let go yet!

I tell you, my joy knew no bounds and my faith was exploding! I decided to pursue it further. I was still missing my health card, blank cheques and cash.

Of course, everyone was very excited with me about the amazing answer to prayer, but many of them thought I was going a bit too far in pursuing it, but they humoured me.

I declared, *"I am calling back my health card, blank cheques and cash. They are my property and God knows where they are."* I refused to budge. I was absolutely convinced that, like David, I would pursue and recover all!

And David enquired at the LORD, saying, Shall I pursue after this troop? shall I overtake them? And he answered him, Pursue: for thou shalt surely overtake them, and without fail recover all.

I Samuel 30:8 KJV

These items were on top, easily visible!

As time passed, I continued to stick to what I had declared. Several weeks later I received another call from a business in the area that had also been robbed. *"Are you missing a health card and some blank cheques?"* he asked. I told him about finding my purse and he was excited to be able to return the missing articles to me. It seemed incredible to him that these items were in the dumpster after all this time, and the dumpster had been emptied numerous times during that period. And these items were on top, easily visible! Again, the angels were watching over them and causing an honest person to come into contact with them!

My faith was growing by leaps and bounds. I decided to go even further! I prayed, *"Dear God, help this person to get caught and be brought to justice and receive help. He obviously has a real problem."*

The thief is caught!

By this time all my friends and many of my relatives had heard the story of the guy who just needed money for baby food and diapers. My youngest sister was one of those, and the comment about the baby food and diapers stayed with her.

> **"I just need money for baby food and diapers." Bells went off in her head!**

She operated a bed and breakfast in a beautiful part of Saskatoon, several miles from the church or the restaurant where my purse was found. Weeks later, a young man came to her door asking if he could cut the grass or pull a few weeds. She declined his offer, saying that her husband would take care of it. When he said, *"All I need is money for baby food and diapers,"* bells went off in her head! And he matched the description of the man I had described to her.

She told him, *"On second thought, why don't you come back at 4 o'clock and I'll call my husband in the meantime and check with him."* And that put in motion a chain of events that caused him to get caught!

Now honestly, what do you think would be the chances in a city the size of Saskatoon, Saskatchewan, Canada, for this man to end up at my sister's home? You and I know that's literally impossible in the natural. I chuckle when I imagine the angels prodding him down one street and up another and finally nudging him into my sister's yard. And what about causing him to use that familiar phrase about the baby food and diapers? If he hadn't used those words, she would not have made the connection!

Years later, I am still amazed at how God responds to faith-filled words. This entire incident was such a faith builder for me, and whenever I share it, it inspires others to step out in faith and believe God to do the impossible for them.

CHAPTER 8

Arrangements for Vehicles

My first faith project

It was January of 1989 and I was traveling home with friends from a conference in Minneapolis, Minnesota. It was a long drive to Saskatoon in a winter blizzard. Sitting in the back seat in the dark, I replayed in my mind the things that I had heard that week. The speaker had taught about what faith really is and gave examples from scripture. He shared a scripture that was "the icing on the cake."

> *Jesus Christ the same yesterday, and today, and forever.*
> Hebrews 13:8 KJV

> I had no difficulty believing that if I had lived back then, that Jesus would have done a miracle for me. But would He do it today?

As stated earlier, I was raised in a Christian home and loved God all my life. As a matter of fact, my dad was a pastor until I was ten years old. He held daily devotions with the family. Although the denomination in which I was raised didn't teach about miracles, I am most grateful for the solid foundation that was laid in my life.

I always knew God *could* do miracles, but I didn't know of anyone who had actually experienced one. As a child, I often thought how wonderful it would have been to be alive during the time that Jesus was on the earth. I had no difficulty believing that if I had lived back then, that Jesus would have done a miracle for me. But would He do it today? The scripture says that He hasn't changed. As I meditated on everything I had seen in scripture, and the testimonies I had heard, faith began to stir in my heart.

I was in great need of a vehicle and I had prayed for one, but not with the kind of understanding that I had received during the week. Actually, it had been more wishful thinking and hoping than believing that God would give me the desires of my heart.

As the miles passed in silence, my spirit and my mind were having an unspoken conversation. I decided I was going to go out on a limb and trust God to provide a car for me and no one was going to talk me out of it. I determined to stake my claim and not deviate from that even in the slightest.

Once I made up my mind, I began to formulate a picture of what the car would look like so I would recognize it when I saw it. I "placed my order," with the Lord. Here's the description of the car that I was expecting to receive.

- Mid-sized car, white in color
- Sporty look
- Teal and magenta splash on the side
- Four doors
- Automatic
- Grey interior
- Nice stereo with cassette player (CD's weren't popular yet)
- Good gas mileage
- No loan required
- Personalized license plate

I was determined to "prove" God faithful. My part was to stay in faith and not cancel the order with the words of my mouth or thoughts of doubt. I decided I would not waver.

> I made a decision not to waver.

Months passed and I can honestly say that as time went on, I was as excited as if the car were already in my driveway. All my friends knew exactly what my car looked like. Often they would tell me they had seen my car driving around town. I knew it was out there. I continually talked about it, looked for it, and imagined myself driving it.

A year passed and then a year and nine months and it still hadn't arrived. I didn't give up—I had come too far to quit. I still didn't know how God was going to do it, but I was convinced He would. The car we had at the time was on its last leg.

Then on a Sunday afternoon that summer, we were driving in the city before the evening church service, when we were broadsided by a large truck. Neil's door took the impact. The first thing we did was hold hands and made the following declaration. *"We pray that there will be no lasting injury and that we will come out ahead financially as a result of what the enemy tried to do."* And we thanked God for sparing our lives. Amazingly, we walked away from the accident with no cuts.

> After talking for a while, the salesman admitted that it was a bit embarrassing for them because this car had been sitting on the lot for a year and nine months and wouldn't sell!

After the police attended the scene, a friend picked us up and took us to church as the car was no longer drivable. Now we *really* needed that car! Rather than be discouraged, I knew that the answer to my prayer must be around the corner, because God knew we had need of a vehicle!

A friend suggested that we needed to go out and look for the car, not just expect it to come to us. So that's what we did. We knew what it looked like, so that narrowed our search considerably.

You see, I could easily have missed it at this point, because I was somehow thinking that God would just park it on my driveway. We must not put God in a box and tell Him how He's supposed to do it. He's a God of variety!

We visited numerous dealerships, where salesmen tried to sell us various cars that didn't fit the description. We insisted it had to be white and had to fit the rest of the criteria.

Eventually we narrowed it down to one dealership—they had a car that fit the description except for one thing. It didn't have the hot pink and teal splash on the side.

After talking for a while, the salesman admitted that it was a bit embarrassing for them because this car had been sitting on the lot for a year and nine months and wouldn't sell! Remember, it was a year and nine months since I began to declare that God would provide the vehicle for which I had placed my order by faith.

Even though everything looked like this was the vehicle, we said we would think on it and return in the morning. We arrived first thing in the morning, only to find that the car was gone! It sat there for a year and nine months, and now when we decided to take it, it's gone! A couple had come in and decided to take it, on the condition that their present car would sell by noon hour.

The salesman wanted us to put in a higher offer, but we refused. We told him if that's the car for us, it will be back here by noon; if not, it isn't the right one. We were going to make sure that this was the right car.

We returned at noon, and the car was back! It looked promising. The salesman was eager to sell. And because it had been sitting on the lot that long, and new models were continually coming in, the price was greatly reduced!

There was just one thing, I told him. No hot pink and teal splash on the side, and the car that I have in mind has that. *"No problem"* he said. *"Just draw us a picture of what you want and we'll put it on the car!"*

This is where I could easily have missed it again, thinking that the splash had to already have been on it. God hadn't said that. My confession was that it would have a hot pink and teal splash, but not that it already had to be on the car when we saw it!

And there was one added surprise! The car had air conditioning! God is good! I had ordered it during a blizzard, so I hadn't even thought of that!

This was a huge confidence builder for me in learning to trust God and take Him at His Word! But you see, I had to first be convinced that God is good, that He delights in blessing His children, and that He wants to give us the desire of our heart.

But here's a qualifier. Before I ever "placed my order" for this car, I had determined to get more intimately acquainted with God and to learn to walk by faith. I was seeking the Blesser, not the blessing. And all that year and nine months while waiting for the manifestation, I developed a relationship with Him that built my confidence and trust. I wanted *Him*, and I knew that these "other things" would follow.

> *But **seek ye first** the kingdom of God, and his righteousness; and all these **things** shall be added unto you.*
> Matthew 6:33 KJV (Emphasis mine)

And that's how I completed my first big faith assignment. I had many opportunities to abort it, or to doubt it, or to even question whether I had heard from God in the first place.

Arrangements for a new truck

It was the year 2000 and we were in need of a new truck for Neil's work. The one we owned at the time was in need of replacement. It didn't heat properly in the winter, and it was quite old, but a new truck was definitely not in our budget at the time.

I recall clearly the day, early in that year, that we decided to make it a faith project instead of just wishing for it.

By this time Neil had a mental picture of what the truck would look like. It was a Chevy Silverado 4x4 with extended cab.

Each time our truck gave us difficulty, I thanked God for the old truck and declared that it was blessed and would work fine for us and for the next owner too. And it did.

Throughout the year, we talked often about our new truck and how wonderful it would be. We didn't tell other people about it— it was *our* faith project. Of course we had many opportunities to give up, but we didn't let go of our confidence. Occasionally we'd visit a dealership to have a look.

About two weeks before Christmas of that year, we made a trip to Calgary from our home in Cochrane and as we pulled onto the highway, I told Neil, *"You know, I just have this feeling that our truck is almost here—like it's just around the corner."* We still didn't have the money to purchase it and we had decided we wouldn't go into debt for it. Yet we really felt that it was on its way. We didn't know how, but that wasn't our concern. We were going to trust God to provide it in whatever way He planned.

On Christmas Day, our family was at our home for the holidays and my mother-in-law was also visiting from Saskatoon. Suddenly the doorbell rang. Who would be at the door on Christmas Day? Besides, all our close friends and relatives never used the front door. Who could it be?

We opened the door and to our great surprise, a brand new 2001 Chevy 4x4 Silverado truck with extended cab was parked on our grass! It was *exactly* like the one we had imagined! It had huge red bows on it!

The friends who stood at the door handed Neil the keys to the truck. We were in shock! Their entire family was in the box of the truck, joyfully singing, "We Wish You a Merry Christmas!" Can you imagine? We had to pinch ourselves to see if we were dreaming. Even though we believed for it, we had no idea how God would provide, and so it came as a wonderful surprise!

Because it was the Christmas season and the registries office was closed, it was several days before we could license the truck and take it for a drive, but it was definitely worth the wait! Various family members took turns sitting in the truck during those days, just enjoying the awesome miracle that enfolded before our very eyes. What a blessing it was to have a new, reliable vehicle without making a single loan payment! It reminds me of a scripture.

> *The blessing of the Lord, it maketh rich, and he addeth no sorrow with it.*
>
> Proverbs 10:22 KJV

In 2011, I was given a new-to-me Jeep by a lady I had never met. She sold it to me for a dollar just to make it legal. No one had ever sat in the back seat. It was in amazing shape.

And other members of our family have also received vehicles, as well as members of our church. At last tally, I counted six people who had vehicles given to them, and two of them received twice!

God cares about our desires, as you will see by the next story.

Arrangements to answer a child's prayer

Spencer, our first grandchild was six years old and really wanted a little motorcycle. Our son, Chris, enjoyed motorcycles too, but we never knew that our little grandson wanted one.

His parents didn't have the finances to purchase it, but they didn't want to discourage him, so they told him *"That's a good faith project."* However, we didn't know any of this until much later.

In the meantime, Chris had a very strong desire to get Spencer a little motorbike. He told us that when he was a young boy, he dreamed of having one. Sometimes he even dreamed that he had it! When he awoke, he ran out to the garage only to find that it had been a dream. His thinking was that every little boy should have a motorcycle! He also didn't know of Spencer's faith project, so I know God was making arrangements by putting this urgency in Chris' heart to find the right motorcycle.

He searched in magazines and ads of all kinds to find a used one, but all to no avail. People who had one didn't want to sell—they just kept it in the family for the next child to use.

One day Chris said *"I'm just going to go out and buy a new one."* He did the research and found just the right bike, a brand new Yamaha PW50.

Chris' younger sister, Melanie, and Neil and I chipped in and purchased a matching helmet, gloves and sweater with rubberized elbows.

Spencer's parents told us later that Spencer had come out of his bedroom that Sunday, dressed for church and announced *"Well, I'm getting my motorbike today!"* Shocked, they asked how he knew. They didn't even know! He replied, *"Because it's Sunday!"* I believe that the Lord ministered to him that his prayer was answered.

The following Thursday, the family got together to surprise him with the motorbike. By this time Spencer's parents had been filled in.

It was such a joy to watch him learn to ride the bike in the alley behind their home, and to see the shock and longing on the faces of his young friends.

Later he told his parents that one of his friends had said, "*Your Mom & Dad must be real rich!*" Spencer told them *"No, you just pray and ask God and you can have one too!"*

God cares about our desires, whether we're young or old. His greatest desire is just to be believed.

CHAPTER 9

Arrangements to Prevent Drowning

It was a very warm day in June of 1983, and my 15 year-old daughter and her cousin had a day off from school. They went to Saskatoon to have their hair permed and I was to pick them up around 5:30 after I got off work.

I stopped in at home to see if the two younger children wanted to come along, but for some reason they wanted to stay home. Looking back, I see how God had made arrangements to spare their lives too. I had already turned onto the highway when it started to rain quite heavily. Although I was a very experienced driver, I just had an inner impression that I should go back and pick up Neil from the jobsite. I'm so thankful I heeded that still, small Voice.

In no time at all, the rain was so heavy the windshield wipers could hardly keep up. The hail was so heavy that it was difficult to hear what we were saying to each other. By the time we got to Saskatoon, traffic was backing up. I took the off ramp at the Husky House on Idylwyld Drive and the car stalled. The water was about six inches deep. Because of the intense hail and rain, everyone just stopped to wait out the storm.

In about five minutes, I felt my feet getting wet, and in just a few more minutes we noticed that the car was floating and bumping into the car in front of us. In minutes, the water had reached our knees and we knew it was time to get out of the vehicle. We noticed that a large manhole on the hillside had blown out and a huge fountain of water was shooting about ten feet into the air. Neil opened his window and climbed out into chest-deep water. He helped me out the same window. The water was like ice; as a matter of fact, the hail was floating on top of the water. The current was so strong, it was difficult to stay upright. Gasping for breath and trying to protect myself from the hail, unable to see properly, I got disoriented and headed the wrong way—into the deep. Neil pulled me back and we fought our way toward the embankment. By the time we reached the top, our car was under ten feet of water!

The rain was so heavy that the storm sewer system couldn't hold the deluge. As a result, the underpass was flooded. We were on the ramp which wasn't nearly as deep. Now I could see why the Holy Spirit had prompted me to go back for Neil, and why the children hadn't wanted to come with me. Thank God for the Holy Spirit!

When we got to the top of the embankment, we realized the chain link fence was locked with a large padlock. The only explanation that I can think of is that Neil had angelic assistance to tear that lock off the gate. We crossed the parking lot in waist deep water, trying to get to the Husky House to use a payphone.

When we got inside, it was crowded with people waiting out the storm. When we walked in, they laughed because we were so very wet. We tried to tell them what was happening out there, but no one believed us. We tried to call the police, but all the lines were jammed.

In the meantime, our daughter and her cousin were waiting outside downtown for us to pick them up and we had no way of reaching them, as cell phones hadn't been invented yet. All we could do was pray that they were okay, and they were, although their lovely hairstyles were rained out!

It was hours before a relative was able to get to us by taking various side roads and eventually we were able to pick up the girls.

It wasn't until much later that evening when we got home, that we realized the seriousness of the situation we had been in. One lady lost her life in the underpass. How we thanked God that He had made arrangements for me to have Neil along, and that He spared us from drowning.

By the next afternoon, the water had receded enough for the tow-truck driver to attach a cable to our car and pull it out. It was so full of mud, sewer and water that it was a total loss. The stereo was packed with mud. During the week while we waited for the insurance adjuster, we went to see the car and found that weeds were already sprouting in the mud on the back seat.

This experience reinforced in us the importance of listening to that still, small inner Voice—the voice of the Holy Spirit who was trying to make arrangements to spare our lives.

CHAPTER 10

Arrangements For You!

Perhaps you've got unanswered questions like so many people do.

- Why do things never seem to work out for me?
- Why haven't I been able to get married?
- Why haven't I been able to have a child?
- Why am I so confused?
- Why are bad things always happening to me?
- Why am I on this earth?
- Does God really have a plan for my life?
- Is there a way out of my situation?
- Why do I seem to go one step forward and two steps back?
- I'm an insignificant nobody. Can God use me?
- Have you had someone throw cold water on your dreams?
- Have you suffered criticism or belittling by someone who should have protected you?
- Have you been falsely accused?
- Have your motives been called into question?
- Have you been cheated out of what was rightfully yours?
- Have you been betrayed by someone in a position of authority?
- Have you found yourself in an impossible situation, one that you can't change?

- Have you experienced deep depression and hopelessness?

If you've ever had any of those thoughts, I've got great news for you! I can provide you with proof that you are constantly in God's thoughts and He *does* have a plan for you! If you don't find out what that plan is and fulfill it, you are missing out on the very reason why God placed you on this earth. You are *not* an insignificant nobody! You are a masterpiece designed by the Creator of heaven and earth and there's no one else like you! No one else can be exactly what you are designed to be. You are on assignment on this earth.

God is still the same today as He was back then! His name is I AM, not "I was" or "I will be." Jesus is still performing miracles today and I can personally testify of many in my life.

Several years ago my pastor challenged the congregation to read through the entire Bible in the coming year. Most people start out great but get bogged down in the genealogies, so he provided a reading schedule that included daily portions from the Old Testament including Psalms and Proverbs, and portions from the gospels and letters to the churches. By following this daily outline, we would complete the entire Bible in one year.

Being familiar with the *King James Version* since childhood, I decided to read the *Amplified Bible* version. Pen in hand, I made notes in my Bible as I read each day. I was amazed at how the Bible came alive. I saw things I had never seen before even though the passages were familiar to me.

It was an awesome experience, so the following year I decided to read *The Message* version. Again, it was like reading a new book. Some days I found it difficult to put it down because it was so fascinating, but the story that changed my life was the story of Hannah.

Have you ever read a portion of scripture, even one that was familiar, and suddenly it's as if the words are lifted off the page and stand out from the rest of the verses? It seems as if it's highlighted. When that happens, God is making that portion come alive to you so that He can minister to you for your particular situation or give you insight for someone else. Perhaps it's just a phrase in a sentence, or even just one word, but whatever it is, it will change your life if you receive it.

That's what happened to me as I read the account of Hannah in I Samuel chapter 1 in *The Message*. The phrase that stood out to me as I read was ***"God began making the necessary arrangements in response to what she had asked."*** That sentence became the motivation for this book.

Suddenly it hit me! When we pray in faith and believe that God hears us, He immediately begins to make the necessary arrangements in response to what we ask! But often we abort our answers by what we do or say afterward.

But I'm getting ahead of myself in my eagerness to share the story in the way it was ministered to me as I read.

> Hannah could have cried all her life and never received a child, but when she got into faith, God began to make arrangements for her!

Hannah's story is told in I Samuel chapter 1. Hannah was married to Elkanah, who loved her very much; however, he had a second wife who made Hannah's life miserable. She had children and Hannah did not. To be barren in that culture carried a stigma. Although her husband loved her, he didn't understand her desire to have a child. He thought she should be happy just being his wife. As a matter of fact, he asked her, *"Oh Hannah, why are you crying? Why aren't you eating? And why are you so upset? Am I not of more worth to you than ten sons?"*[23] He always gave an especially generous helping of food to her because he loved her so much and because God had not given her any children. He meant well, but comfort food wasn't what she wanted or needed! She wanted a child.

To make matters worse, *"her rival wife taunted her cruelly, rubbing it in and never letting her forget that God had not given her children. This went on year after year. Every time she went to the sanctuary of God she could expect to be taunted. Hannah was reduced to tears and had no appetite."*[24]

It's one thing to be taunted in the work place or elsewhere, but in church? Unthinkable. And you'll see it wasn't only her rival that did it—the priest or "pastor" falsely accused her!

It's not unusual for other people, even Christians, to make harsh or cruel judgments when we are going through difficult situations. They don't know all the facts, and we don't understand why things are happening the way they are or what we can do about it.

It's also human nature to blame God when things aren't going well. Hannah could have cried all her life and never received a child, but when she got into faith, God began to make arrangements for her!

Don't blame God for your situation. I grew up believing that whatever happens in our lives is God's will. I just took that as "gospel truth" and never really studied the scriptures with an open mind to see if that was the truth.

I've heard people blame God for the death of a loved one when He had nothing to do with it. God gets blamed for sickness, for disasters, and even hurricanes and such are called "acts of God."

I've even heard people blame God in cases where a person died while driving drunk! God had nothing to do with that.

---

23 I Samuel 1:8 The Message

24 I Samuel 1:7 The Message

Let's say that you're the parent of a much-loved child who contracted a terrible disease and died a horribly slow and painful death. You did everything in your power to assure the child of your love and took advantage of every treatment available to save the life of your child, but the child died.

All your friends and loved ones know how much that child meant to you and how you would have done anything for the child. But suddenly everyone blames you. After all, you let it happen. You didn't stop it. Absurd, you say, but that's exactly how many people treat God!

Jesus came to this earth to make us whole, to give us His peace. The Hebrew word for "peace" is shalom[25] which literally means there is nothing missing, nothing broken, nothing lacking.

John 10:10 clearly states what Jesus does and what the devil does.

> *The thief does not come except to steal, and to kill, and to destroy. I have come that they may have life, and that they may have it more abundantly.*
>
> John 10:10 NKJV

Take the example of a teenager whose father has warned him repeatedly not to speed, but he does and is killed. Who in their right mind would say it was the fault of the father? Eventually we have our own will and God will not cross it! The freedom to choose is the most powerful thing that He gave us.

Yet religion has taught us that whenever something bad happens to a person, somehow God is at fault because He "let it happen." If something good happens, they attribute it to luck.

Hosea 4:6 says that God's people perish for a lack of knowledge and it's the truth. I shared earlier how this lack of knowledge

---

25 Strong's Concordance 7999 - Hebrew, Shalom

To be safe in mind, body or estate; well; happy; to be completed; to make good; friendly; to perfect; make to be at peace; make prosperous; make restitution; restore; reward.

could have caused me to become a young widow if God hadn't made arrangements for me to get understanding of what He is really like! But I'm getting ahead of myself again! Slow down, Ruth!

Back to Hannah. It was the time of the year when the family made their annual trip to Shiloh to worship and offer a sacrifice to God. She always dreaded it because of the taunting and ridicule she endured from the other wife, and because it was a constant reminder that she had no children.

Let's look in on her now. The situation is so desperate that she decided to seek some solitude by slipping away to the sanctuary to pray. In the quietness, away from the ridicule, she did something she had not done all the other years she had come. She poured out her heart to God and made Him a promise.

> *Crushed in soul, Hannah prayed to God and cried and cried—inconsolably. Then she made a vow: Oh, God-of-the-Angel-Armies, if you'll take a good, hard look at my pain, if you'll quit neglecting me and go into action for me by giving me a son, I'll give him completely, unreservedly to you. I'll set him apart for a life of holy discipline.*
>
> I Samuel 1:9-11 The Message

Hannah thought God had been neglecting her! Although Hannah didn't realize it, she was setting into operation plans for the next prophet of Israel!

We too can visit our future in prayer! God has already been in our future, and when we turn our lives over to Him and give Him permission to work, we can put marvelous things into motion that aren't yet fully revealed. But His plan is always for good.

> *For I know the thoughts and plans that I have for you, says the Lord, thoughts and plans for welfare and peace and not for evil, to give you hope in your final outcome.*
>
> Jeremiah 29:11 Amplified

Remember, a father who abuses a child should end up in prison. That's the law. God designed it that way for the protection of children. How can we possibly think that God would abuse His precious children to "teach them a lesson?" He would then be the author of confusion and divided against Himself.

But Hannah had limited knowledge of God's nature. She thought He was neglecting her by not giving her children. The truth was that God wanted to give her a child and when she came into agreement with His plan, He began to make arrangements according to what *she* said!

> Her response to a false accusation positioned her for a miracle!

But, just like with us, the enemy will try to get us to abort our dreams, and that's what happened with Hannah. Here she is in church, a place where she should feel safe! Wounded and vulnerable, she's pouring out her heart to God with such depth of feeling that she can only mouth the words. Perhaps she doesn't have the strength to speak, having wept to the point of exhaustion. Or maybe she didn't want to take a chance on being overheard. But God heard every word she prayed.

The priest watched her suspiciously and jumped to the conclusion that she was drunk. Can you imagine how she must have felt to have her "pastor" misjudge such a sacred moment? She could so easily have aborted the whole thing if she had taken offense. And unfortunately, that's where people most often miss it.

> *It so happened that as she continued in prayer before God, Eli was watching her closely. Hannah was praying in her heart, silently. Her lips moved, but no sound was heard. **Eli jumped to the conclusion** that she was drunk. He approached her and said, "You're drunk! How long do you plan to keep this up? Sober up, woman!"*
>
> I Samuel 1:12-14 The Message (Emphasis mine)

Her response to a false accusation positioned her for a miracle! And the same thing can happen to you if you'll keep your heart right in every situation.

See how respectfully she responds and how this actually brought correction to the priest.

> *Hannah said, "Oh no, sir—please! I'm a woman hard used. I haven't been drinking. Not a drop of wine or beer. The only thing I've been pouring out is my heart, pouring it out to God. Don't for a minute think I'm a bad woman. It's because I'm so desperately unhappy and in such pain that I've stayed here so long."*
>
> *Eli answered her, "Go in peace. And may the God of Israel give you what you have asked of him."*
>
> I Samuel 1:15-17 The Message

Peace means wholeness. He came into agreement with her. He was actually saying, "Be whole; nothing missing, nothing broken, nothing lacking."

> *"Think well of me—and pray for me!" she said, and went her way. Then she ate heartily, her face radiant.*
>
> I Samuel 1:18 The Message

She could so easily have responded by saying, *"I'll never darken the door of that church again. I'll never trust another pastor."* And in so doing, she would have cancelled God's plan that had already been put into motion.

> People say, *"I'll believe it when I see it."* Faith says, *"I'll see it when I believe it."*

This world is full of wounded Christians who no longer attend church because they got offended or were spiritually abused and never got past the hurt. If you are reading this book and find yourself in that situation, please hear my heart. I've been where you're at, and I understand. That's why I wrote this book. But I've got hope for you! I didn't stay there, and you don't have to either!

Previously, Hannah refused to eat and had a long face but now she did the opposite. Yet nothing had changed in her outward situation. She was still childless, still being taunted by her husband's other wife. But in her heart, she had already received her child. Her words and actions gave witness to the fact that she had received it by faith! Her faith had corresponding actions!

I wonder what the other wife's reaction was to Hannah's new demeanor. No amount of taunting could take away Hannah's confidence.

People often say, *"I'll believe it when I see it."* Faith says, *"I'll see it when I believe it."*

> *Up before dawn, they worshiped God and returned home to Ramah. Elkanah slept with Hannah his wife, and **God began making the necessary arrangements in response to what she had asked.***
>
> I Samuel 1:19 The Message (Emphasis mine)

Wow! God started making arrangements! How sad that many of His arrangements are aborted because of murmuring, doubt or bitterness.

I believe that even as you are reading this book, God is waiting for you to step out in faith so that He can begin making arrangements for *your* breakthrough! Whatever you believe for is being birthed in you *now*!

The only qualification is that it must line up with God's Word and with His character. I once heard of someone who prayed to marry a certain woman, but she was already married to someone else. God will not hear a prayer like that because it doesn't line up with His Word. He can't go against His Word, but He is looking for people who will simply take Him at His Word and act on it.

The eyes of the Lord search the whole earth in order to strengthen those whose hearts are fully committed to him.

2 Chronicles 16:9a NLT

But if you're submitted to God and want His best for you, you won't want anything that's contrary to His Word.

And Hannah kept her promise to God! We must make sure that we don't forget God when He comes through for us.

God is Making Arrangements

Hannah wanted a boy child but was taunted day after day,
So she sneaked off to the sanctuary to pour out her heart and pray.
The priest wasn't very discerning; "You're drunk," is what he said.
She could have gotten offended, but presented her case instead.

When he came into agreement, she went on her way so blessed,
Because God began to make arrangements according to her request!
Peter was in the dungeon; John the Baptist just lost his head;
But God made arrangements according to what the prayer group said.

Jonah's rebellion cost him a lot when into the sea he was thrown;
But God arranged for a gigantic fish to provide for him a home.
Marinated in digestive juices and wrapped in seaweed and kelp,
God made arrangements to throw him up in response to his cry for help!

Is your situation hopeless? Are you facing fear or pain?
Have you experienced failure and loss, and your health you haven't regained?
Then give God something to work with! Get your tongue in line with His Word,
So He can make arrangements according to what He heard!

©Copyright by Ruth Hamm

The password to your situation

The Lord drew something to my attention in the Message Bible in my daily reading. I was reading Psalms 89 and round about verse 15, this is what it says.

> *Blessed are the people who know the PASSWORDS of praise, who shout on parade in the bright presence of God.*

Then in Psalms 100, it appeared again! Now He really had my attention!

> *On your feet now—applaud God!*
> *Bring a gift of laughter, sing yourselves into his presence.*
> *Know this: God is God, and God, God.*
> *He made us; we didn't make him. We're his people, his well-tended sheep.*
> *Enter with the PASSWORD: "Thank you!"*
> *Make yourselves at home, talking praise.*
> *Thank him. Worship him.*
> *For God is sheer beauty,*
> *All-generous in love, loyal always and ever.*

> Psalms 100 The Message (Emphasis mine)

Just think! You have the secret password—the key you need to turn your situation around!

Have you ever tried to enter a certain website but forgot your password? No matter what you did, it wouldn't allow you to enter without the password. Sometimes it's as simple as using lower case instead of upper case, or sometimes you've just simply for-gotten the password. You just can't enter that site until you get the correct password! The only way you can get it (if you haven't written it down somewhere) is to click on *forgot your password* and have them email it to you.

Perhaps you're at a place in your life right now where you feel like you've tried everything but it's just not working. *"What am*

I doing wrong?" "Where did I miss it?" It used to work, but it's not working anymore.

You feel like you've hit a wall, like the door to heaven is locked, like the heavens are brass, and God's forgotten your name. Nothing could be further from the truth!

I believe God has a word for you today! God doesn't have to email you the password; He was far ahead of that technology—He put it in writing thousands of years ago, and kept it protected from viruses, crashes, meltdowns or hackers.

What you focus on will develop!

Losers look at what they're going *through*, while winners look at what they're going *to*! Thoughts are simply previews of coming attractions—negative or positive. I heard someone put it this way—if it's on your mind, it's in your future!

> God will anoint a certain verse just for you, and it becomes your PASSWORD for a particular situation. It's a *rhema* word from God for you at that time.

Let me caution you at the start that there's a danger in mentally "tuning out" something you've heard before. I know this from personal experience. A wise Bible teacher once taught me always to listen to the Word that's being taught as if I've never heard it before. It's human nature to tend to "tune out" something we've heard before.

I recall reading a scripture for the umpteenth time and suddenly *seeing* something I never did before. You see, God will anoint a certain verse just for you, and it becomes your PASSWORD for a particular situation. It's a *rhema*[26] word from God for you at that time. It's a word that's alive and energized and powerful! If you receive it that way, God will use it to give you direction to victory!

26 The spoken word of God as opposed to *logos*, which is the written word of God.

But remember, your understanding of it and the resulting decisions you make must line up with the Word and the character of God.

Just open your heart right now to see what password God will give you for your situation. You can do that by simply inviting the Holy Spirit to reveal His thoughts to you. Make a daily habit of reading a portion of Scripture; after all, the Holy Spirit is the Author, and He can explain things to you and direct you through the reading of His Word. Take *heed* to what His Word says to you as you read. To heed means to "lean over to pay close attention." It means "earnest, continued inspection."

God is not an assembly line Creator. He likes originals and He creates masterpieces. He takes this to the extreme—even to the degree that no two snowflakes are alike! Many of the things He invented are still being discovered, although they've been around from the beginning.

> One example is DNA—now there's a password! The Word confirms this when it says that "the blood cries."

One example is DNA—now there's a password! The Word confirms this when it says that the Lord told Cain *"Your brother's blood cries out to me from the ground!"* In other words, blood speaks. And when DNA was finally discovered, it confirmed that fact. That password alone has solved thousands of crimes, but was unknown until the fifties!

Now in order for you to be reassured that He really cares about you personally and wants to help you, let me give you a few scripture references that you can study so that you'll become convinced.

> Faith is a strong persuasion based on what you've heard. Faith is simply what you believe.

Faith is simply a strong persuasion based on what you've heard. If you haven't heard the truth about God, you're convinced He

---

might hurt you. Or perhaps you're convinced that He will do it for someone else, but not for you. In order to trust someone, you have to be convinced that they have your best interests at heart. So get convinced!

- Your name is written in the palm of His hand. Isaiah 49:16
- He holds you by the right hand. Psalms 18:35
- He is your buckler. He stands between you and the enemy. Psalms 18:2
- He is your hiding place. Psalms 32:7
- He is your comfort. 2 Corinthians 1:3
- He saw and planned all your days even while you were in your mother's womb. Psalms 139:13
- He wants to see your face and He loves your voice. Song of Solomon 2:14
- He will never forsake you. Hebrews 13:5
- His plans for you are for good and not evil. Jeremiah 29:11
- He is leading you into all truth. John 16:13

The ***password of praise*** opens doorways and brings provision into dry places.

> *Sing to God, sing praises to His name, **cast up a highway for Him Who rides through the deserts**—His name is the Lord—be in high spirits and glory before Him!*
> Psalms 68:4 Amplified (Emphasis mine)

> An attitude of praise has nothing to do with circumstances.

We are told to come into HIS PRESENCE with praise and thanksgiving. We should live a life of praise and thanksgiving all the time. Begin today to make a habit of starting each day by being thankful for even the smallest things. If you need financial provision, be thankful for every penny you have and every penny you find. Thank Him for even the smallest improvements in your situation, and do it even before you see any change! Ask God for "seed" or finances to sow. Be generous with whatever you have.

> *For God is the one who provides seed for the farmer and then bread to eat. In the same way, he will provide and increase your resources and then produce a great harvest of generosity in you.*
>
> **2 Corinthians 9:10** NLT

Don't you just love it when your children are thankful for something you've promised them even before they get it? That's how our Heavenly Father wants us to respond to His promises even before we see the manifestation.

An attitude of praise has nothing to do with circumstances. It's a choice! It doesn't depend on our present situation or circumstance. Everything is subject to change when we live a life of praise and thankfulness.

I'm going to share an example where praise prevented suicide and brought about household salvation!

I'm going to share an example where praise prevented suicide and brought about household salvation!

There's a wonderful example in Acts chapter 16 that demonstrates how the password of praise broke chains and unlocked doors. You'll see how the praises of Paul and Silas not only brought about their own freedom, but many others were delivered and it brought household salvation to the man who imprisoned them!

What doors do you need opened? Is there someone in your family or sphere of influence that needs to have chains broken? Then read on!

The judges went along with the mob, had Paul and Silas's clothes ripped off and ordered a public beating. After beating them black-and-blue, they threw them into jail, telling the jailkeeper to put them under heavy guard so there would be no chance of escape. He did just that— threw them into the maximum security cell in the jail and clamped leg irons on them.

*Along about midnight, Paul and Silas were at prayer and singing a **robust hymn** to God. The other prisoners couldn't believe their ears. Then, **without warning**, a huge earthquake! The jailhouse tottered, **every door flew open**, all the prisoners were loose.*

Acts 16:22-26 The Message (Emphasis mine)

Notice, they weren't quiet! They were in pain from the beating, their feet were in stocks, and moreover, they were innocent!

Because Paul and Silas used the password of praise and focused on God instead of themselves, look what happened! There's no doubt that things would have turned out differently if they had focused on their beating and the injustice done to them. They would have become depressed, discouraged, thinking God had forsaken them. They could have thought, *"Here we were, just doing God's work. Things were going so well; we got Lydia and her whole household saved and baptized, cast the devil out of that girl. Then we got falsely accused and the judges went along with the mob. God, where are you?"*

But the fact that they began to PRAISE and pray, not only provided the way out of their situation, but also the way out for others. Look what happened!

Startled from sleep, the jailer saw all the doors swinging loose on their hinges. Assuming that all the prisoners had escaped, he pulled out his sword and was about to do himself in, figuring he was as good as dead anyway, when Paul stopped him: "Don't do that! We're all still here! Nobody's run away!"

The jailer got a torch and ran inside. Badly shaken, he collapsed in front of Paul and Silas. He led them out of the jail and asked, "Sirs, what do I have to do to be saved, to really live?" They said, "Put your entire trust in the Master Jesus. Then you'll live as you were meant to live—and everyone in your house included!"

They went on to spell out in detail the story of the Master—the entire family got in on this part. They never did get to bed that night. The jailer made them feel at home, dressed their wounds, and then—he couldn't wait till morning!—was baptized, he and everyone in his family. There in his home, he had food set out for a festive meal. It was a night to remember: **He and his entire family had put their trust in God;** *everyone in the house was in on the celebration.*

Acts 16:27-34 The Message (Emphasis mine)

*He who **heeds** instruction and correction is not only himself in the way of life but also is a way of life for others. And he who neglects or refuses reproof not only himself goes astray but also causes to err and is a path toward ruin for others.*

Proverbs 10:17 Amplified (Emphasis mine)

Another way to describe "heed" is to "get a grip."

Other people's victories are dependent on YOU! I have heard it said that a mother is like the rudder of a ship. If she's not happy, no one is happy. She sets the tone in her home to a large degree.

Do you set the tone in your environment? What about your place of employment? Does your attitude set the tone there? Is it an attitude of praise or murmuring? Do your family members, your co-workers, your friends and church family see you as someone who lights up a room or as someone who spreads sadness and gloom?

Notice that in both of these situations, Lydia and the jailer, there was household salvation! Another example is the story of Zacchaeus.

> *Jesus responded, "Salvation has come to this home today, for this man has shown himself to be a true son of Abraham.*
>
> Luke 19:9 NLT

> **If you're believing for household salvation, praise is a necessity!**

Praise is a password! If you're believing for household salvation, praise is a necessity! Don't focus on what is, but on what will be! Neil and I have experienced tremendous breakthroughs while raising our children by using the password of praise to change situations.

Why do you think the Holy Spirit recorded this event for us? The Bible says that all these things were given as examples. The purpose is to show us God's character, His power, His willingness, and to demonstrate that His ear is open to praise!

Is your situation so hopeless that you need an earthquake to shake it loose to give you some room to breathe again?

> **God will create a fault under your mountain if you praise Him and don't quit!**

It took faith for them to sing praises, sitting bent over in stocks, bleeding and beaten after having their clothes ripped off and given a public beating! This didn't happen in private—they were humiliated first and then beaten and imprisoned.

Even those things didn't rob them of their song or their faith! I tell you, God will create a fault underneath your mountain if you will praise Him in faith and not quit! Let me prove it to you!

*For **I will be leaning toward you with favor** and regard for you, rendering you fruitful, multiplying you, and establishing and ratifying My covenant with you.*
Leviticus 26:9 Amplified Bible (Emphasis mine)

Don't you just love it when you overhear someone saying nice things about you? Well, so does God! The Bible says that God watches and listens in on our conversations when we are talking about Him and respect Him! It gets His attention!

I like the way it's worded in The Message Bible in Malachi 3:16-18 (Emphasis mine)

*Then those whose lives honored God got together and talked it over. God **saw** what they were doing and **listened in**. A book was opened in God's presence and **minutes were taken** of the meeting, with the names of the God-fearers written down, all the names of those who honored God's name.*

*God-of-the-Angel-Armies said, "They're mine, all mine. They'll get **special treatment** when I go into action. I treat them with the same consideration and kindness that parents give the child who honors them.*

*Once more **you'll see the difference** it makes between being a person who does the right thing and one who doesn't, between serving God and not serving him."*
Malachi 3:16 The Message. (This is an easy verse to remember–it's one of the 3:16's.)

What were they doing when it says they got together and talked it over? They were talking about God! That's another way of praising Him! Saying nice things about Him!

And God was taking minutes! That's amazing! As someone who has taken minutes of business meetings for many years, I know why minutes are important! One reason is so that there's an accurate and permanent record of what took place. I've often wondered, does God like to re-read our conversations because it makes His heart glad, or does He show it to others to share the joy?

If you're not convinced yet, I'll give you a few more.

> **God looked down** *from heaven upon the children of men to see if there were any who understood, who sought (inquired after and desperately required) God.*
>
> Psalms 53:2 Amplified Bible (Emphasis mine)

> *For the eyes of the Lord run to and fro throughout the whole earth to show Himself strong in behalf of those whose hearts are blameless toward Him.*
>
> 2 Chronicles 16:9 Amplified Bible (Emphasis mine)

> *Behold, the Lord's eye is upon those who fear Him [who revere and worship Him with awe], who wait for Him and hope in His mercy and loving-kindness.*
>
> Psalms 33:18 Amplified Bible (Emphasis mine)

> *The eyes of the Lord are toward the [uncompromisingly] righteous and His ears are open to their cry.*
>
> Psalms 34:15 Amplified Bible (Emphasis mine)

> *For the eyes of the Lord are upon the righteous (those who are upright and in right standing with God), and His ears are attentive to their prayer.*
>
> I Peter 3:12a Amplified Bible (Emphasis mine)

> *Sing to God, sing praises to His name, cast up a highway for Him Who rides through the deserts—His name is the Lord—be in high spirits and glory before Him!*
>
> Psalms 68:4 Amplified Bible (Emphases mine)

Praise casts up a highway in a dry place. Any situation where there is lack is a dry place, whether it involves health, relationships, finances or employment.

Murmuring is a sign of ingratitude!

A desert is a place where there's no provision; a person can die there from lack of water or food. A person can get lost there because there's no direction. But praise constructs a HIGH way for God to come to your desert and rescue you. He can create an oasis that provides a place of refreshing for others who are in the desert!

Refrain from *murmuring* for it was what kept the children of Israel in the desert for 40 years instead of 11 days! Murmuring is a sign of ingratitude.

> *Neither murmur ye, as some of them also murmured, and were destroyed of the destroyer. Now all these things happened unto them for examples: and **they are written for our admonition.***
>
> 1 Cor. 10:10, 11 KJV (Emphasis mine)

> *Jesus therefore answered and said unto them, Murmur not among yourselves.*
>
> John 6:43 KJV

> *And the men, which Moses sent to search the land, who returned, and made all the congregation to murmur against him, by bringing up a slander upon the land.*
>
> Numbers 14:36 KJV

> *Yes, they spoke against God: They said, "Can God prepare a table in the wilderness?"*
>
> Psalms 78:19 NKJV

I was reading in Leviticus about the different animals the children of Israel could and couldn't eat, and I noticed something I had not seen before.

He told them that, among other birds, ravens are unclean animals and they shouldn't eat them. Yet God used ravens to deliver the food to Elijah! So don't get any preconceived ideas on how God will solve your problem. Leave that to Him because His way of thinking is so superior and He's never short of ideas!

What is the enemy trying to steal from you?

I encourage you to give yourself a check-up to see if there's an area in your life where the enemy has an inroad. God wants us to take advantage of every benefit that was purchased for us at such a great cost.

Jesus said that He gave us His peace. The word "peace" does not mean the absence of turmoil, but rather the kind of peace or tranquillity that comes from being whole—nothing missing, nothing broken, nothing lacking. It means that we can be at rest and at ease while going through a difficult time because we are hidden under His wings and we know the outcome!

Perhaps it's not a personal item that's been stolen from you—it could be something else, like your health or reputation, your children, favour or finances. Get in line with God's Word and pursue the enemy and get back what was taken from you.

Now let me give a word of wisdom at this point. There are some things you won't be able to recover. For example, the death of a loved one, or the death of a marriage if there's been a re-marriage. But you can claim restoration of how it affected you.

Take time to learn about your covenant rights if you are a believer. You are not demanding anything from God—you are enforcing the return of what rightfully belongs to you.

If you are not yet a believer, you can become a member of the family of God in just a few minutes. Then you will be entitled to all the privileges of a child of God. He loves all His children the same. He does not play favourites with His children—but He does respond when they talk like He talks!

Please pray the following prayer with all sincerity, and "trust" God with all your heart.

Dear God, I come to You through Jesus, Your Son. I acknowledge that I am a sinner in need of a Saviour. I accept Jesus as my Saviour, recognizing that He died to purchase me. Thank You for cleansing me and giving me right standing with You, as if I never sinned! I give you complete access to my life and hand over the control of my life to You. Help me to live for You. In Jesus' Name, Amen.

If you prayed that prayer, welcome to the family of God! Let me encourage you to find a good church where you can grow in your Christian life. Ask God to help you. You are His child and He is so in love with you. He wants the best for you in every area of your life. Talk to Him every day, and expect Him to talk to you!

May I suggest you read the books of Matthew, Mark, Luke and John in the New Testament, in order for you to get acquainted with Jesus. He is the same today as He was yesterday, and He will be that way forever. He will never hurt you. Welcome to a wonderful new life. You are a brand new creation!

As you read this book, my prayer is that you've been inspired and that you've made a determination to do great exploits for God! I also pray that God will use you to help make arrangements for others to get to know God in a more personal way.

May you enjoy His presence and power in your life!

To order more copies of this book,
contact the author at:

House of Ruth Publishing
P.O. Box 1787
Cochrane, AB
T4C 1B6
Canada

TEL: 403-932-1150
EMAIL: houseofruth@shaw.ca